by WENDY SMEDLEY & ABY GARVEY

THE ORGANIZED
& INSPIRED | SCRAPBOOKER

EXPERT ADVICE

PROJECTS

QUIZZES

INSPIRING
SCRAPBOOK SPACES

THE ORGANIZED & INSPIRED SCRAPBOOKER
by Wendy Smedley and Aby Garvey

2007 EDITION

Editorial
SENIOR EDITOR Ali Monson
MANAGING EDITOR Angie Lucas
FOUNDING EDITOR Stacy Julian
EDITOR IN CHIEF Lin Sorenson
ASSOCIATE EDITOR Rachel Gainer
ASSISTANT EDITOR Elisha Snow
EDITORIAL ASSISTANT Carolyn Jolley
COPY EDITOR Jenny Webb

Design
ART DIRECTOR Claudia Daniels
CREATIVE DIRECTOR Cathy Zielske
PHOTOGRAPHY
AMERICAN COLOR: Brian Smith, Symoni Johnson

Production
SENIOR PRODUCT MANAGER Dana Wilson

2010 EDITION

Editorial
EDITOR IN CHIEF Jennafer Martin
MANAGING EDITOR Lara Penrod
SENIOR EDITOR Kim Jackson

Design
ART DIRECTOR Erin Bayless
DESIGNER Marin Barney

EDITOR IN CHIEF Susan White Sullivan
QUILT AND CRAFT PUBLICATIONS DIRECTOR Cheryl Johnson
SPECIAL PROJECTS DIRECTOR Susan Frantz Wiles
SENIOR PREPRESS DIRECTOR Mark Hawkins
PUBLISHING SYSTEMS ADMINISTRATOR Becky Riddle
PUBLISHING SYSTEMS ASSISTANT Clint Hanson
MAC INFORMATION TECHNOLOGY SPECIALIST Robert Young
CHIEF EXCUTIVE OFFICER Rick Barton
VICE PRESIDENT AND CHIEF OPERATIONS OFFICER Tom Siebenmorgen
DIRECTOR OF FINANCE AND ADMINISTRATION Laticia Mull Dittrich
VICE PRESIDENT, SALES AND MARKETING Pam Stebbins
SALES DIRECTOR Martha Adams
MARKETING DIRECTOR Margaret Reinold
CREATIVE SERVICES DIRECTOR Jeff Curtis
INFORMATION TECHNOLOGY DIRECTOR Hermine Linz
CONTROLLER Francis Caple
VICE PRESIDENT, OPERATIONS Jim Dittrich
COMPTROLLER, OPERATIONS Rob Thieme
RETAIL CUSTOMER SERVICE MANAGER Stan Raynor
PRINT PRODUCTION MANAGER Fred F. Pruss

The Organized & Inspired Scrapbooker is published by Leisure Arts, Inc., 5701 Ranch Drive, Little Rock, Arkansas 72223-9633. 501-868-8800. www.leisurearts.com.

This product is manufactured under license for Creative Crafts Group, LLC., Creative Crafts Group company, publisher of Creating Keepsakes® scrapbook magazine. ©2010. All rights reserved.

Jennafer Martin, *Creating Keepsakes*

A Leisure Arts Publication

Library of Congress Control Number: 2010931964 | ISBN-13/EAN: 978-1-60900-087-5

ABOUT THE AUTHORS

WENDY SMEDLEY

As creative editor for *Simple Scrapbooks* magazine, Wendy Smedley is always on the cutting edge of product trends and industry news. She manages the product-focused section of the magazine and represents *Simple* on the popular *Scrapbook Memories* program seen on local PBS stations.

Wendy officially entered the scrapbook industry in 1996, and in her 10 years of experience, she's been involved in every aspect of the hobby—from retail to manufacturing and distribution to public relations to her current editorial post. She's also a seasoned teacher and has made numerous local and national television appearances.

She's the author of two editions of *The Complete Idiot's Guide to Scrapbooking* and has been helping to shape the *Simple Scrapbooks* vision since the magazine's inception in 2002.

Wendy and her husband, Kent, live in Centerville, Utah, with their five boys, Taylor, Justin, Jacob, Nathan, and Caden.

Thanks, Aby, for your faith in my abilities, for your inspiring friendship, and for rescuing me from my cluttered space. I'm excited to see what's in store for us next! Thanks to the *Simple Scrapbooks* team for their encouragement and support. Thanks, Kent, for cheering me on—and my five boys for letting me take their pictures (most of the time).

ABY GARVEY

Aby Garvey is an organizing expert and founder of simplify 101, a professional organizing business she runs with her husband, Jay. Using the skills she honed during her 13 years in the corporate world, Aby helps her clients streamline their daily activities and create orderly, inspiring spaces. She has a bachelor's degree from Michigan State University and an MBA from Southern Illinois University–Edwardsville.

Aby loves working with scrapbookers because she is one herself. She understands the importance of fitting the hobby neatly (and beautifully!) into your home and life. She's the author of an e-book titled *The Happy Scrapper: Simple Solutions to Get Organized and Get Scrapping* and shares her organizational tips in a monthly simplify 101 e-newsletter. Aby also teaches classes about time management and goal setting at bigpicturescrapbooking.com.

Aby and her husband, Jay, live in Edwardsville, Illinois, with their two children, Collin and Kailea.

Thanks, Wendy, for your shared vision, your sense of humor, and your friendship. I couldn't imagine a more perfect collaborative partnership. Thanks, Jay, for being a brilliant business partner and an incredible father to our children. And thanks, Collin and Kailea, for your giggles, your snuggles, and your love.

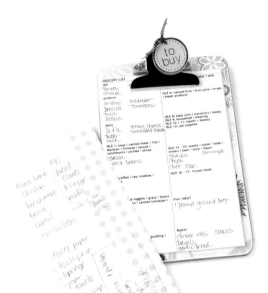

WRITING THIS BOOK HAS BEEN AN ADVENTURE, ESPECIALLY SINCE WE LIVE MORE THAN 1,300 MILES APART! BUT THANKS TO CELL PHONES, ONLINE SHARED DOCUMENTS, AND OUR "ORGANIZED AND INSPIRED" APPROACH, WE WERE ABLE TO MAKE IT HAPPEN!

If we're being honest, generally Aby is the organized one and Wendy is the inspired one. But we've definitely rubbed off on each other, learning valuable lessons that we're dying to pass on to you. Maybe the best way we can describe what it was like to work together is to tell you about a trip we took to the grocery store.

During a working vacation at Aby's home near St. Louis, we decided that we'd each be in charge of a meal for the weekend, so we headed to the grocery store. Aby shopped from a printed shopping list, which she sorted in order of each aisle's contents and carried around on a decorative clipboard. Wendy, on the other hand, followed a list scribbled on a used envelope, casually gathering up ingredients and placing them in her cart as she navigated the unfamiliar grocery store. When we met at the checkout, we were both a bit surprised at how well the other's method had worked!

After the shopping trip, we took turns in the kitchen. Guess who followed a detailed recipe to cook up her grandmother's Swedish meatballs,

carefully measuring and checking the instructions? And guess who casually poured the ingredients for her favorite tortilla soup into a crockpot without even glancing at a recipe? Despite our opposite approaches to preparation, we both ended up with delicious meals.

Our cooking experience illustrates the differences in our perspectives and personalities. Not only do we prepare meals differently, we also have opposite approaches to scrapbooking. We loved learning from each other—Wendy's creative vision helped to inspire Aby's disciplined approach, while Aby's ability to organize gave Wendy's haphazard spontaneity a bit of (creative) structure.

We are living proof that there is no right way to scrapbook (or cook!). Your scrapbooking approach is probably different from both of ours, too—and that's okay. In fact, it's fantastic! Because we're not here to tell you how to scrapbook. We're here to help you discover how scrapbooking fits into your life—so you can create an organized, personalized workspace that inspires you to keep going!

While we think this book is pretty darn pleasing to the eye, it's not meant to be a coffee table book. No, this book is designed to inspire you to action—action that will help you discover organizing methods, storage systems, and maybe even an entirely new perspective about scrapbooking.

We're not here to give you every conceivable organization and storage option on the planet. Instead, we want to show you some of our favorites— and, more importantly, to teach you how to decide what works for you. We believe inspiration is a big part of that process, so we'll help you make purposeful, inspired decisions so you can create a workspace that matches your vision and goals.

In section 1, we'll walk you through the eight components of a scrapbook and offer specific organization and storage solutions for each element.

In section 2, we'll give you an up-close look at the workspaces of a few successful and productive scrapbookers. Plus, you'll learn how to select and incorporate the right organizing strategies for your space and your lifestyle.

In section 3, we'll roll up our sleeves and get to work on inspiring projects for your workspace.

And throughout the journey, we'll ask you to dig deep and answer the questions in the chapter quizzes that will inspire you to create real and lasting change in your scrapbook space!

Are you ready to create the organized and inspired workspace that you and your hobby deserve?

Pick up a pen, and let's dive in!

Wendy   Aby

contents

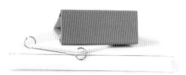

SECTION

1

PIECE BY PIECE

Have you ever thought about just how many components it takes to create one scrapbook layout? You've got photos, stories, products, and tools, to name a few. Each serves a unique purpose in your memory-saving hobby, and each needs its own organized and inspired place in your workspace.

Getting ORGANIZED

READY FOR AN ORGANIZED, EASY-TO-USE SCRAPBOOKING SPACE? THE FACT THAT YOU'RE READING THIS BOOK TELLS US THAT YOU JUST MIGHT BE. MAYBE YOUR STASH OF PRODUCTS IS BEGINNING TO TAKE OVER ALL THE AVAILABLE SPACE IN YOUR SCRAP AREA.

Maybe you spend more time searching for tools and embellishments than you spend actually scrapbooking. Maybe you're just ready to make sense of all your stuff. Regardless of your reason for picking up this book, we're glad you're here! And we're ready to help.

But before we jump into the specifics about exactly how to create a fun, practical (and inspiring!) scrapbooking space, let's get one thing straight. Storage and organization are not the same thing. They're often used interchangeably, but they're actually quite different in both purpose and function.

In the plainest sense of the word, "storage" simply means the act of putting items away for future use—perhaps inside boxes, on bookcases, in hanging files, or in jars. But this is just one small part of organization. Just because you've tucked away everything you own in neat, properly labeled containers, that doesn't necessarily mean you're organized.

Being truly organized means that yes, you have storage solutions in place, but those storage solutions actually help you accomplish your goals. It means that you have an overall sorting system, customized to your specific needs and creative preferences, that tells you:

①How to categorize and group things together
②Which things go in which container
③Where each container goes in your organizational plan or room scheme

Sound hard? It's really not, as long as you know where to start. And that's where we come in.

In this book, we'll guide you through the decision-making process for both organization and storage, helping you select systems that will work for you and your unique approach to scrapbooking.

pens

We know you're excited to dig into your supplies, but before you do, let's do a quick overview of the basic organizing process we'll use throughout this book. Each of the nine chapters in section 1 is centered on a single component of scrapbooking: inspiration, approach, photos, stories, tools, etc. We apply the same universal principles of organization in each chapter to help you:

① Create your vision
② Select an organizing method
③ Organize and pare down
④ Store and display

Then our fun and helpful quizzes (found at the end of each chapter) will guide you to action.

❶ CREATE YOUR VISION

Defining your vision involves deciding how you want things to function when you're done. Whether you're organizing your entire space or focusing on just photos and supplies, decide how you want things to be different from the way they are now. Think in terms of benefits—how the changes will help you work better and feel more excited about your hobby.

❷ SELECT AN ORGANIZING METHOD

Your organizing method depends a great deal on what you're working with, whether it's photos or memorabilia or stories. So we'll walk you through this process chapter by chapter, offering specific ideas for each element of scrapbooking. But here's a list of general organizing methods you can choose from.

Organize by activity. Store your tools and supplies based on how they are used. This process allows you to create zones within your space so every activity has a home.

Organize by topic. Sort your products or photos by topics such as events, holidays, themes, and seasons. Storing by topic makes it easy to grab and go if you scrapbook at crops or at a temporary workspace like a kitchen table.

Organize by manufacturer or product line. If using a complete line simplifies your scrapbooking process, or if you think about products in terms of their manufacturer, then keeping entire product lines together will make scrapbooking easier.

Organize by color. If color is a driving force in your creative process, and if you think in terms of colors when creating layouts, then consider arranging all your supplies (or even your photos) in color groups.

Organize by project. Keep everything you need for a single project—including photos, papers, embellishments, and tools—all in one place. This method can save you time when you actually sit down to scrapbook your chosen project since all of your supplies are within easy reach.

Organize by pattern, shape, or mood. If you tend to look for products based on shape or style, consider sorting by categories like "polka dots," "stripes," "happy," or "romantic."

Organize chronologically. If you scrapbook your photos chronologically, chronological organization may be an effective method for your other items as well. (Gather Valentine's Day–related supplies in a folder labeled "February," for example.)

As we move forward into other chapters, keep in mind that you don't have to use the same organizing method for every component. It will vary from item to item, based on your vision, your space, and your process.

❸ ORGANIZE AND PARE DOWN

Once you've decided on your organizing method for a particular item in your scrapbook stash, it's time to gather everything together. If you have a scrapbooking space, empty it—or at least remove the items you're organizing. Set up a "staging area" using boxes, zipper-top bags, and sticky notes to sort, categorize, and label your items as you are sorting them. Once you have everything in its proper group, decide which things you want to keep and which things no longer suit your tastes or your goals.

TIP Finding a charity you feel great about helping makes filtering out scrapbook supplies that much easier. Look for organizations such as day care centers, schools, retirement centers, and nursing homes. One of our favorite charities is Operation Scrapbook, an organization that uses donated scrapbooking supplies to provide scrapbooks for foster children and hospice patients. If you're in angst over the money you spent on these unneeded supplies, host a swap with friends or sell items at a garage sale or on eBay.

❹ STORE AND DISPLAY

Once you have your stash pared down and organized, it's time to choose storage containers and decide where to keep them in the context of your larger scrapbook space. Here are four basic options to consider for storing your scrapbooking tools and products:

OPEN AND VISIBLE
For items that inspire you visually, use visible storage solutions such as baskets or bins that sit open in your workspace. These storage solutions and their contents will add a decorative and inspiring element to your space.

OPEN AND NOT VISIBLE
An open but opaque container stored on
a shelf or in a cubby allows easy access to
its contents while maintaining the visual
continuity of a closed container.

words

pens

ta

CLOSED AND VISIBLE

A glass jar allows you to see everything you have
at a glance, making it a suitable storage solution
for items you love to look at. But if you find these
containers visually distracting, consider putting them
behind cabinet doors or a curtain.

CLOSED AND NOT VISIBLE

A solid container with a lid or other closure will keep things organized but out of sight. This solution is helpful if you're easily distracted by visual clutter or if you're storing items that are visually uninspiring to you.

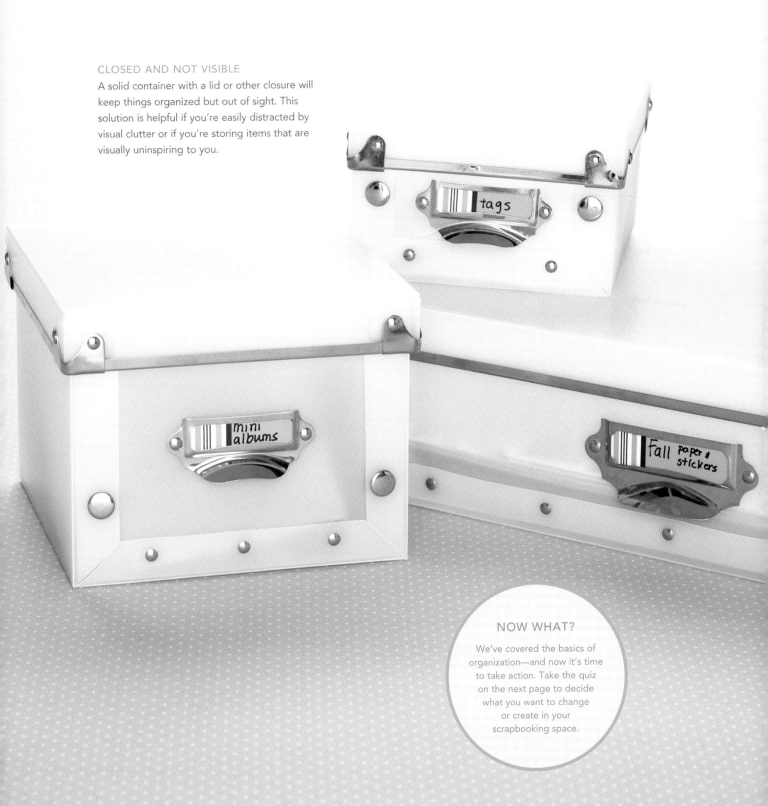

tags

mini albums

Fall paper & stickers

NOW WHAT?

We've covered the basics of organization—and now it's time to take action. Take the quiz on the next page to decide what you want to change or create in your scrapbooking space.

CHAPTER (1) QUIZ

ORGANIZATION

YOUR VISION

① What prompted you to pick up this book? Or in other words, what do you want to change and why?

....
....
....
....

② Ideally, how will things look when you're done organizing?

....
....
....
....

③ How will your scrapbooking space function when you're done organizing?

....
....
....
....

ORGANIZING METHODS

④ Check the organizing categories you are currently using, and circle the ones that you feel are working the best for you. Cross out any that you know don't fit your style.

☐ Activity

☐ Topic

☐ Manufacturer/product line

☐ Color

☐ Project

☐ Pattern, shape, or mood

☐ Chronological

⑤ Check the types of storage solutions you are currently using, and circle the ones that you enjoy using the most. Cross out any that you know don't work for you.

☐ Open and visible

☐ Open and not visible

☐ Closed and visible

☐ Closed and not visible

⑥ Do you need to see your things to remember what you have, or do you find visual stimulation distracting?

....
....
....

⑦ Are you naturally inclined to tidy up your space and put things away when you're done with a project, or do you like to leave things out?

....
....
....

⑧ Do you prefer a space where all the containers match, or do you prefer an eclectic mix of containers?

....
....
....

RECAP

The questions in this quiz are designed to help you start thinking about what you want to change or create in your scrapbooking space. Then, with this information in mind, you can seek out ideas in the rest of the book that will help you implement the organizational and storage solutions that will help you create your vision.

Read over your answers to the quiz to become aware of the types of storage solutions that appeal to you. Which organizing categories and storage solutions are you using that already work well for you? Are there any you'd like to try out? For example, if you said you need to see your supplies to remember what you have (question 6), but you keep everything in closed boxes, you could experiment with storage solutions that allow your supplies to be visible.

If it's easy for visual "stuff" to distract you, read up on storage solutions that hide clutter and present a unified face.

If you aren't naturally inclined to tidy up your space when you're done scrapbooking, look for storage solutions that are easy to load and unload, like open containers or drawer units where the drawers are easy to pull out and carry over to your workspace.

If you aren't sure if you prefer a mix of containers, let us help! Browse section 2 of this book and consider which spaces appeal to you the most. Wendy and Aby (chapters 10 and 11) use a mix of containers, whereas Beth's space (chapter 12) uses fewer types of storage solutions. Renee and Kelli's spaces (chapters 15 and 14) allow you to have the best of both worlds by keeping open containers behind closed doors.

CHECKLIST

- Start forming your vision for a more organized approach to scrapbooking.

- Decide on which organizing schemes you'd like to investigate in the pages ahead.

  ☐ Activity

  ☐ Topic

  ☐ Manufacturer/product line

  ☐ Color

  ☐ Project

  ☐ Pattern, shape, or mood

  ☐ Chronological

- Read the applicable chapters for each scrapbooking element before deciding how to reorganize your things. Then follow these steps:

  ☐ Organize

  ☐ Pare down

- Select storage containers.

  ☐ Open and visible

  ☐ Closed and visible

  ☐ Open and not visible

  ☐ Closed and not visible

Getting INSPIRED

WHETHER IT COMES TO YOU IN THE FORM OF STORIES, EMOTIONS, OR CREATIVE IDEAS, INSPIRATION IS ULTIMATELY WHAT MOTIVATES EACH OF US TO SCRAPBOOK. YOUR BIG-PICTURE INSPIRATION IS THE GRAND IDEA OR PHILOSOPHY OR SPARK THAT INSPIRED YOU TO BEGIN SCRAPBOOKING IN THE FIRST PLACE—AND THAT KEEPS YOU GOING TODAY.

Your day-to-day inspiration is what motivates you to sit down and create a specific scrapbook layout or project.

In this chapter, we'll explore the concept of inspiration as a driving force behind your scrapbooking and share ideas that will help you make it a more consistent part of your creative process.

You're probably wondering: What does inspiration have to do with organization? We're glad you asked! A key component to organizing is **being intentional about what you bring into your space and your life.** Knowing what inspires you—what made you want to create scrapbooks in the first place and what keeps you inspired throughout the creative process—makes organizing a natural, sustainable process.

The more aware you are of the reasons you scrapbook, the easier it is for you to navigate through all the choices you face: which photos to use, which products to buy, how to organize your stuff, what stories to tell, and so on. Identify what truly inspires you and drives you and it will become your ultimate filter, laying the foundation for everything else. You can easily eliminate clutter by cutting out the supplies and ideas that get in the way of what you really want to accomplish.

Before we dive into organization and storage specifics for the things that inspire you, let's look at how to incorporate inspiration into your scrapbook projects and your scrapbook space:

① Become more aware of what inspires you
② Gather inspiration
③ Select an organizing method
④ Store and display your ideas

❶ BECOME MORE AWARE OF WHAT INSPIRES YOU

In order for inspiration to produce all of its amazing results, it's important to become aware of what inspires you and why. Ask yourself: Is my hobby inspired by a love for my family? Or is it driven by my desire to be creative? It doesn't matter how you answer those questions. What matters is that you know the answer so you can keep your scrapbooking focused on what inspires you.

❷ GATHER INSPIRATION

Once you understand your sources of inspiration, you can start collecting inspiring ideas and objects to incorporate into your projects and scrapbook space. Browse through magazines, jot down ideas, and look around your house. Gathering inspiring ideas in one place is key to making your scrapbooking meaningful, because your inspiration collection can help you keep your hobby focused on what matters most to you.

❸ SELECT AN ORGANIZING METHOD

Your ideas are useful only when you can find them easily in a pinch, so having a functional system to organize inspiration is a must. The goal is to sort your ideas based on what, specifically, inspires you about the object or idea. There are endless ways to organize inspiration pieces, but here are a few of our favorites. Hopefully they'll help you discover your own system.

Organize randomly. That phrase may sound like a contradiction, but just bringing all of your ideas into a single location is one form of organization. Having ideas grouped together this way can help when you're completely stuck or feel like you need a general inspirational boost.

Organize by category. Organize your inspiration and ideas into categories, such as design ideas, color options, techniques to try, products to buy, photography tips, and so on. For instance, if you tend to get stuck in a color rut, having a bulletin board packed with examples of inspiring color usage may help ignite your creative spark.

Organize by project. Another option is to categorize inspiration and ideas by specific projects—including projects that are already underway and those that are still in the planning stages. For example, if you're planning a 50th anniversary album for your parents, collect all of your ideas for the project into one place, which will make the creative process much easier when you're ready to start working.

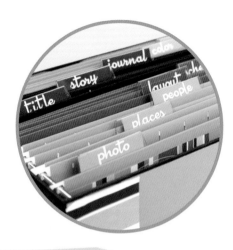

❹ STORE AND DISPLAY YOUR IDEAS

Once organized, your ideas can continually inspire your scrapbooking if you display them in accessible, or even visible, storage containers. Here are a few of our favorite storage solutions for organizing ideas and inspiration pieces:

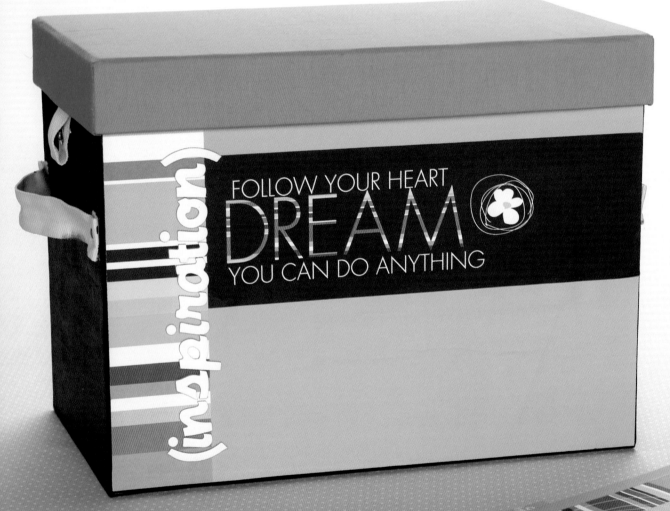

BOX FILE AND FILE FOLDERS

Don't overlook this basic storage workhorse. If files are a natural part of your other (non-scrapbooking) organizing systems and they work well for you, they may just make a great system for scrapbooking ideas as well. Set up file folders using any of the organizing solutions mentioned, and file away. To personalize a standard filing system, consider embellishing your file folders with inspiring designs, colors, and accents.

DISPLAYS

Instead of tucking three-dimensional inspiration pieces away in a box, display them as part of your workspace décor (or elsewhere in your home). This type of visible storage serves as a constant reminder of the reasons you scrapbook and can be used as a rotating display for various items you love.

BOOKS, BINDERS, NOTEBOOKS, AND MAGAZINE HOLDERS
Storing your ideas in a binder, notebook, or journal is another effective storage strategy. Binders offer you the flexibility of rotating ideas around and easily removing those that you've used or that no longer appeal to you. And many are small enough to fit into a bag for capturing ideas on the go. Using magazine holders, you can easily fill standard three-ring binders with intact publications—if you just can't bear to tear your favorite periodicals apart. (Note: Notebooks and journals require the use of staples or adhesive to attach items to pages, but they allow you to write thoughts and impressions directly on the pages.)

photography

design

story

color

JUMP RINGS

Use a jump ring to group inspiring items together in one neat and tidy place. Simply glue or staple your items onto index cards, or hole-punch them so you can attach them directly to the binder ring. Fill up your inspiration ring with images from magazines, cool clothing tags, fabric swatches, paint chips, etc.

NOW WHAT?

We've covered the basics of inspiration and how it drives scrapbooking—and now it's time to take action. Take the quiz on the next page to discover what inspires your hobby.

CHAPTER (2) QUIZ

INSPIRATION

① Why did you start scrapbooking?

....

....

② What do you love most about scrapbooking today?

....

....

③ Which of the following elements is most important to you? (Check it off.)

☐ Stories (your journaling and words)

☐ Photographs

☐ Scrapbook supplies

☐ A means for creative expression

④ When reading a scrapbooking magazine or idea book, which is most interesting to you?

☐ Page topic or story ideas

☐ Photography tips

☐ Seeing new products

☐ Seeing other scrapbooker's layouts and learning new design techniques

⑤ Which parts of scrapbooking are easiest and most fun for you?

☐ Capturing life via written words

☐ Capturing life via photographs

☐ Shopping for and incorporating fun supplies onto my pages

☐ Designing and creating scrapbook pages

⑥ List five things or people that inspire you:

creatively	emotionally or spiritually
①	①
②	②
③	③
④	④
⑤	⑤

visually	to scrapbook
①	①
②	②
③	③
④	④
⑤	⑤

RECAP

Knowing what inspires your scrapbooking makes everything else easier. If your answers on the quiz point you in the same direction each time, you're starting to hone in on your inspiration! Look at what you checked for questions 3 through 5. Does one of the following patterns emerge?

You're inspired by stories. To nourish your love for telling stories:

• Pay close attention to the ideas in the stories chapter

• Bring images that inspire you to tell your stories into your home or scrap space (like Wendy's antique typewriter) or create a display shelf for your journals

• Set up a place that inspires you to write and then carve out time in your schedule to write on a regular basis

You're inspired by photos. Celebrate your love for photography by:

• Paying close attention to the ideas in the photos chapter

• Hanging and displaying photos in your scrap space or throughout your home

• Playing with your camera regularly: shoot spontaneous photos of your family, your home, your life

You're inspired by supplies. To fully enjoy your scrapbooking products:

- Pay close attention to the ideas in the products chapter

- Use your scrapbooking supplies to create home décor items

- Store your supplies in visible ways—let them inspire you on a regular basis

You're inspired by the creative process and design. Bring more creativity into your life by:

- Paying close attention to the ideas in the approach chapter

- Collecting and displaying ideas that celebrate your love for design and creating

- Keeping a sketchbook handy: use it to brainstorm new designs and to sketch ideas that catch your eye wherever you are

CHECKLIST

- Become aware of what inspires you. Use the quiz to guide you through the process.

- Look through the items you've already collected or flagged in magazines. What do they represent: story ideas, photo ideas, products to buy/use, or design ideas?

- Look for inspiration—it's everywhere! Try these sources:

  –Cards, gift wrap, shopping bags
  –Magazines and catalogs
  –Color combinations in print, nature, fabric, and paint swatches
  –Designs of product packaging, décor items, clothing, and websites
  –People and relationships
  –Stories, quotes, and things people say
  –Memorabilia
  –Everyday life
  –Feelings of love, joy, gratitude
  –Photos (yours and other people's)
  –Scrapbook products, magazines, and idea books

- Collect ideas and inspiration.

- Set up a system to collect ideas—try a clipboard, notebook, or in-box.

- Organize your ideas and inspiration.

  ☐ By topic

  ☐ By project

  ☐ Randomly

- Decide how to store and display your ideas and inspiration.

  ☐ Open and visible—inspiration board, display shelf, jump ring

  ☐ Closed and visible—glass jar filled with inspiring items

  ☐ Closed and not visible—file cabinet and folders

  ☐ Closed but easily visible—books, binders, notebooks

Once you have your solution, implement it!

ORGANIZED
& INSPIRED

Approach

WHAT'S YOUR APPROACH? WE'RE REFERRING TO YOUR CREATIVE PROCESS—THE STEPS
YOU FOLLOW TO TURN AN INITIAL IDEA INTO A FINISHED LAYOUT OR ALBUM. BUT, TO US,
"APPROACH" MEANS MORE THAN JUST STEPS. WE'RE ALSO INTERESTED IN WHAT DRIVES
YOU THROUGH THE PROCESS, WHERE YOU START, AND WHERE YOU GO FROM THERE.

Can you create beautiful and rewarding scrapbook
pages without consciously knowing how you
got there? Absolutely! If your approach is giving
you the results you want, you've probably never
bothered to dissect how and why it works.

But there are tangible benefits that come from
understanding your approach to scrapbooking:
first, it enables you to set up a space that works
the way you work, and second, it can help you
save one of your scarcest commodities—time!
When you organize and store all your scrapbooking
elements so that they fit your creative process, you
can work faster and more efficiently.

Are you ready to discover your own unique
approach to scrapbooking? We're ready to help.
Here's how to figure it out:
  ①Be inspired
  ②Discover your starting point
  ③See how the other components of your
     scrapbooking approach come together

❶ BE INSPIRED

As we mentioned in chapter 2, your big-picture
inspiration is what motivates you to scrapbook in
the first place, and it also helps you decide which
projects to work on and where to start. As you
define your approach in this chapter, remember
what you've learned about what inspires you—and
let that drive you.

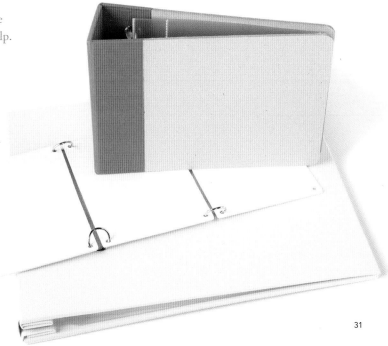

31

❷ DISCOVER YOUR STARTING POINT

While inspiration (however you defined it in chapter 2) is the underlying driver to your approach, you have to start somewhere in order to physically create a page. Do you head for your photos first? Do you scribble down your thoughts? Do you sort through your supply stash before doing anything else? These elements of scrapbooking, along with all the others, can come into play in endless ways and combinations. But to keep things simple, we narrowed the options down to four common starting points:

Design first. A page layout, design scheme (such as those featured in every issue of *Simple Scrapbooks* magazine), color combination, or even a new font can inspire you to create an entire page. Once you're inspired by a design element, consider how you can pull together photos, products, and a story to fuel your inspiration.

Story first. When you start with a story, you create a layout because, above all, you have something to say. Your first step is to scribble your thoughts down or compose them on your computer, while the ideas are fresh in your mind. Once your journaling is figured out, you can move through the rest of the creation process in a variety of ways, but everything else you add (from photos to papers to accents) is meant to enhance the story.

TIP Regardless of your scrapbooking approach, be sure to include a final step: clean up. Getting your space back in shape after each project ensures that your workspace is always ready and waiting for you whenever you're inspired to create.

notes

Photos first. You know that feeling when you're thumbing through a stack of prints and that perfect photo jumps out at you? The minute you see it, layout ideas flood your mind. The inspiration you get from your photo sparks journaling ideas, and from there it's easy to select design elements that let your photo shine.

Supplies first. Scrapbook products are just plain inspiring, some more than others. When you find a product that really calls to you, ideas about exactly how you want to use it can start forming instantly. Whether it's colorful chipboard letters or a fun patterned paper that gets you excited, start there first. The other components of your project can follow in any order to show off the products you love.

❸ SEE HOW THE OTHER COMPONENTS OF YOUR SCRAPBOOKING APPROACH COME TOGETHER

Once you've discovered your typical starting point for a layout or project, it's time to explore where your process moves from there. If you're not sure what comes next, put this book down for 20 minutes and start working on a layout. See what happens naturally—and take note of your approach.

We know there are endless ways to approach scrapbooking. In fact, the two of us are living proof of that! The important thing is to adopt an approach that works for you.

Wendy's approach.
Wendy's approach to scrapbooking is directly tied to her output—so she begins each project with a clear idea of what she wants to accomplish. With an end result in mind (and inspiration driving her), she gathers either photos or products (depending on which component inspires her to create the layout). Journaling, design, and memorabilia follow, bringing her full circle to her desired output.

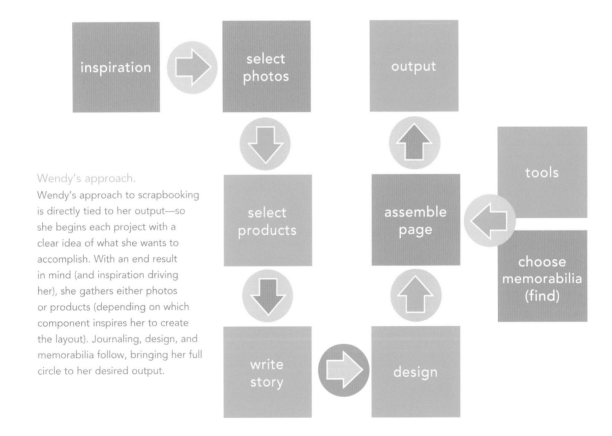

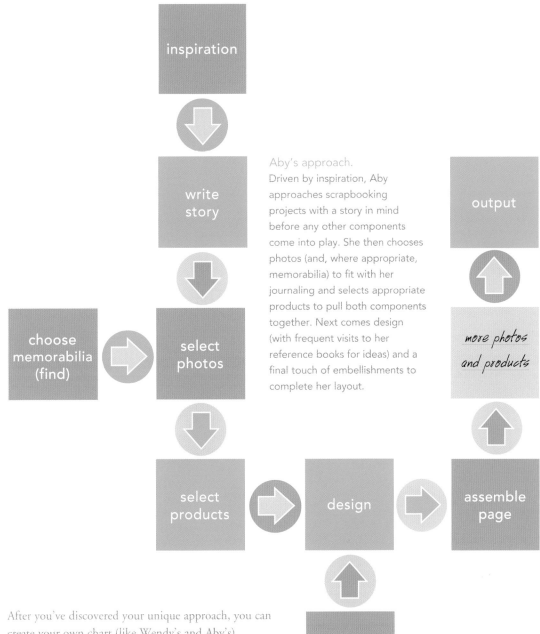

inspiration

write story

choose memorabilia (find)

select photos

select products

design

assemble page

output

reference

more photos and products

Aby's approach.
Driven by inspiration, Aby approaches scrapbooking projects with a story in mind before any other components come into play. She then chooses photos (and, where appropriate, memorabilia) to fit with her journaling and selects appropriate products to pull both components together. Next comes design (with frequent visits to her reference books for ideas) and a final touch of embellishments to complete her layout.

After you've discovered your unique approach, you can create your own chart (like Wendy's and Aby's).

NOW WHAT?

We've covered the basics of making your approach an organized and inspired component of scrapbooking—and now it's time to take action. Take the quiz on the next page to explore your approach to scrapbooking.

CHAPTER (3) QUIZ

APPROACH

Fill in your answers to this questionnaire while creating a scrapbook page.

① What was the inspiration for this particular page, layout, or project?

....
....

② List the steps, in order, you took to create this project.

....
....
....
....
....
....

③ Which step in the process was the most fun for you? Why?

....
....

④ Which step was the least fun? Why?

....
....
....

PHOTOS
⑤ When you selected photos, how did you think of them?

☐ By specific date/chronological

☐ By event

☐ By person

☐ By moment or memory

⑥ Was it easy to find the photos you wanted to use? ☐ Yes ☐ No

STORY
⑦ When you added the journaling and/or title to your page, was it easy to get down on paper what you wanted to say? ☐ Yes ☐ No

⑧ How do you feel about what you wrote down? Are you glad it's there (does it mean something to you), or are you ambivalent about it (for example, it's there because you're "supposed" to have journaling)?

....
....

PRODUCT
⑨ How did you think of or look for the supplies you used in your project? (Check all that apply.)

☐ By color (pink paper, pink ribbon, pink brad)

☐ By manufacturer or line (BasicGrey, 7gypsies)

☐ As "the new stuff I got just for this project"

☐ By theme (Disney, wedding, baby)

☐ By season (fall, winter, spring, summer)

☐ By mood (whimsical, romantic, funky)

☐ By pattern (polka dot, stripe, paisley)

☐ By person or gender (masculine/feminine, boy/girl)

☐ By type of item (chipboard letters, metal attachments)

☐ Chronologically (a specific date or month of the year)

⑩ Was it easy to find the product you wanted to use? ☐ Yes ☐ No

⑪ Which ones were hardest to find?

....
....

TOOLS

⑫ Was it simple to find the tools you wanted to use? If not, why? What would you like to change?

DESIGN/REFERENCE

⑬ Was it easy to decide how to arrange all your elements on your page? If not, what made it hard? What could make it simpler for the next time?

----

⑭ When you approached your design, how did you work?

☐ Sketched out my idea first

☐ Referred to designs by other people/from other sources

☐ Moved things around on the page until they looked right

RECAP

By filling out the quiz while you scrapbooked, you gained a heightened awareness about your approach to scrapbooking. Look back and notice:

Which steps are easiest for you and which are more difficult. For the harder steps, pay attention to the reference chapter. Set up a reference system that makes these steps easier for you. You can also choose to eliminate steps altogether. If, for you, scrapbooking is about photos and the journaling is frustrating and unrewarding, why continue to always include it? For you, photo captions might be all the journaling you need.

How you look for your tools and supplies. This will help you decide the best organizing system for the various elements you use to scrapbook.

Which things were easy to find and which things were more challenging. This will help you prioritize what you want to change—or reorganize—first. Look at questions 11 through 13 for some ideas about where to start.

CHECKLIST

- Continue to pay attention to your scrapbooking approach. The more you learn about how you naturally do things, the easier it will be to organize your things in ways that work well for you.

- Try out some other approaches to see if they work better for you (it could be fun!). Start a page using a different source of inspiration: for example, if you usually start with photos, start with a page concept and then pull together the rest of the elements.

- As you identify areas you would like to work on, note them and read through the sections of the book that deal more specifically with them.

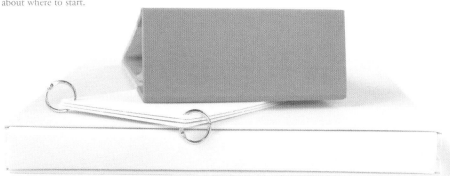

ORGANIZED
& INSPIRED

Photos

CHANCES ARE, PHOTOGRAPHS ARE THE REASON YOU JUMPED INTO SCRAPBOOKING IN THE
FIRST PLACE. YOU WANTED TO DO SOMETHING WITH THAT GROWING PILE OF PHOTOS FROM
YOUR WEDDING, FAMILY VACATIONS, BIRTHDAYS, AND OTHER SIGNIFICANT LIFE EVENTS.

Your photos are a connection to your history, both
recent and long past, and you are eagerly pairing
them with their accompanying stories to preserve
memories for the future.

But if you're as camera happy as we are, you
have way more photos than you know what to do
with, and that can make organizing and storing
all of your pictures quite a task. Whether you're
working with printed pictures or digital files,
developing an organizing strategy is key to making
your photos useful. If you can't easily find the
pictures you're looking for, how are you going to
get them into your scrapbooks?

In this chapter, we'll give you some ideas
for getting your pictures organized and stored
neatly—and accessibly—in your space.

Here's a look at how to incorporate a photo
storage strategy into your organized and
inspired space:
①Be intentional about the photos you take
②Select an organizing method
③Organize and pare down
④Store and display your photos

**❶ BE INTENTIONAL ABOUT THE
PHOTOS YOU TAKE**

Ask yourself: What stories do I want to tell, and
what photos do I need to add to my collection
in order to tell those stories? Let your answers to
those questions help you be selective about when
to snap the shutter. Then be intentional about
which photographs you scrapbook and which
photos you store in other ways.

TIP   Keep your camera in an easy-access place.
When your camera is within reach (with a
charged battery), you're more likely to capture photo-
worthy moments as they happen.

❷ SELECT AN ORGANIZING METHOD

Organize your photos using a system that will allow you to easily access the photos you want to scrapbook. Here are a few of our favorite photo-organizing solutions; we hope one of them will be just the thing you need to get your piles of pictures in check.

Organize by topic. If your approach to scrapbooking relies on overriding themes, try topical organization. You could set up folders or dividers for each of your children, one for family group shots, one for extended family, one for friends, and so on. Or you could try the "library of memories" method taught by Stacy Julian, founding editor of *Simple Scrapbooks* magazine. She sorts her photos into albums titled "places we go," "people we love," "things we do," and "all about us."

people

places

us

things

House stuff
School Treasures
Hand made
Collections
Games
Favorites
Boy Stuff

TIP   It's equally as important to develop a standardized labeling system to help you keep tabs on what you've got. Here's an example of how to label digital files using dates and topics: 2007-01-11-grandma's house

Organize by project. If you tend to dream up future projects while looking through your photos, consider organizing them based on your project ideas. Having all of your photos grouped together this way can save you time when you're ready to begin a project—and it may just inspire you to get moving on your ideas!

Organize chronologically. Chronological photo storage might be a great solution if you prefer to scrapbook your memories sequentially. Sorting photos by year or decade, then by season, will make it easy to get going when you sit down to scrapbook a specific event or significant day.

TIP Even if you sort your photos chronologically, let inspiration drive your scrapbooking. Scrapbook the photos you're inspired by at the moment instead of whatever is next in line. Your pages will reflect this inspiration and passion, and you won't be forced to ignore the great page ideas trapped inside your head.

❸ ORGANIZE AND PARE DOWN

Start by sorting photos into piles (according to date, topic, size, or whatever system you've chosen) so you can later transfer them into your chosen storage solution. Make sure there's a trash pile too. There's no sense saving blurry shots, shots where people's eyes are closed, shots that are very similar to better photos you have, etc. And remember—it's okay to keep only a handful of the best photos from a particular event and throw the rest away.

When you choose which pictures to save (or which to print from your digital files), be realistic. Keep and print only those photos you know you will use—the ones you have a specific project in mind for or those that are just so great that you know you'll find a use for them. If you can't bear to throw any photo away, no matter how un-scrapbookable it is, create a box or file titled "cold storage" and keep your bad photos there until you decide to either toss them out or return them to your organizational system.

Not convinced about paring your photos down? Think about this: if you have 5,000 photos, scrapbooking them all would mean making 714

spreads (if each spread included seven photos), investing $3,570 (if each spread cost $5), and spending 1,428 hours to complete them (if each spread required two hours of work). So can you see why photo filters are so essential? You can't possibly scrapbook every photo you currently have, not to mention those yet to be taken. It's absolutely necessary to create a system to help you filter your photos before you organize and store them.

❹ STORE AND DISPLAY YOUR PHOTOS

Once your photos are organized, it's time to choose a storage solution that makes them accessible. Here are a few of our favorites:

Kent and me over the years— for an "us" album?

PHOTO ALBUMS

Often we view photo albums as a final resting place for pictures. But albums can actually serve as temporary storage for photos—before they are scrapbooked. To make albums work for your photo storage needs, slide your pictures into plastic sleeves and add labels where needed. This option also allows you to show off your pictures while they are waiting to join your scrapbooks.

CD CASES
Consider storing your digital photos on CDs for easy access and portability. Copying photo files onto disks is a way to back up the images saved on your computer—keeping your precious pictures safe from potential data loss and system failures. To jazz up your CD storage, personalize your CD cases with patterned paper, photos, and fun embellishments.

PHOTO BOXES AND OVERSIZED BOXES

Boxes provide easy, thumb-through access to photos. Once you fill them with your sorted pictures, simply label the groupings with cardstock dividers. Add an extra flair of creativity by embellishing the dividers with some of your favorite scrapbooking supplies.

VISUAL PHOTO DISPLAYS

Visible photo storage, such as a magnetic board or a clothespin display, allows you to enjoy your photos before you scrapbook them. Storing your photos in sight lets you easily modify the look of your workspace by rotating the photos—and you may just come up with a way to add them to a layout by simply seeing them in your space.

photo list

1- Jacob
2- Nathan
3- Disneyland trip
4- school
5- Jackson Hole trip
6- Justin
7- Caden

8- Taylor
9- Nathan
10- Camping
11- Wyoming w/ mom
12- Cousins
13- friends
14- Baseball

NOW WHAT?

We've covered the basics of making photos an organized and inspired component of your scrapbooks—and now it's time to take action. Take the quiz on the next page to decide how you will work with and store your photos.

CHAPTER (4) QUIZ

PHOTOS

① What stories do you want to tell with your scrapbooking?

② Think of the photos you already have—what's missing? List the photos (or kinds of photos) you'd like to take to help you tell your stories.

③ When you scrapbook, do you tend to move through your photos chronologically or topically? Or do you think of your photos in terms of their size/how they'll fit together in a layout?

④ If you have 30 photos from one event, what method do you use to sort through them and decide which ones to scrapbook?

- ☐ Pick your favorite one (or two or three)
- ☐ Pick several photos that represent the highlights of the event
- ☐ Focus on finding photos that, together, show everyone who was there
- ☐ Different filtering system

⑤ What's most important to you in storing your photos?

- ☐ Compact, portable storage
- ☐ Backup of digital data
- ☐ Ease of access
- ☐ Being able to share your photos with others, even if they aren't scrapbooked yet
- ☐ Creative displays (to inspire you to scrapbook them!)

RECAP

Use your answers to the quiz to make your decisions about how you will work with and store your photos. What do your answers tell you about the way you like to scrapbook with photos?

For example, if you like to work through your photos chronologically and you also want them stored so that you can still share them with others, you could sort your photos into albums organized by year or seasons within a year.

But if instead you decide you'd like to work through your photos thematically and that you also want them stored compactly but with easy access, you could sort your photos into storage boxes (one for each topic, with sub-topics dividing them up inside).

However you decide to organize your photos, use the opportunity to sort them as a chance to pare them down at the same time—two birds, one stone!

CHECKLIST

Create your vision.
- Make a list of photos missing from your collection that you'd like to take

- Select a photo organizing system (or two!)

  ☐ Chronological

  ☐ Topical

  ☐ Size

Organize your photos.
- Gather up these handy supplies:

  ☐ All your photos

  ☐ A large work surface (it's best if you have one that you can set up and leave undisturbed for a period of time)

  ☐ Sorting containers—small plastic tubs or boxes

  ☐ Trash can

  ☐ Acid-free cardstock to make temporary photo dividers (or sticky notes)

  ☐ Pens for labeling dividers

- Organize based on your sorting method

- Sort items based on the selected method

- For topic-based sorting, use subcategories such as specific people, specific places or trips, and specific things you'd like to chronicle in your scrapbooks

Pare down.
- Place in your trash can photos that are

  ☐ Blurry—and you have better representations of the subject

  ☐ Irrelevant to you

  ☐ Duplicates

  ☐ Redundant—outtakes that aren't meaningful or special

- Label and store!

CHAPTER 5

Memorabilia

ORGANIZED
& INSPIRED

FROM OLD LOVE LETTERS TO HIGH SCHOOL TROPHIES AND CONCERT TICKET STUBS, MEMORABILIA TUGS AT OUR HEARTSTRINGS LIKE NOTHING ELSE CAN. THESE ITEMS HAVE SIGNIFICANCE TO US BECAUSE, LIKE OUR SCRAPBOOKS, THEY CAPTURE THE ESSENCE OF OUR LIVES IN DAYS GONE BY. SO WHY DO WE STASH THEM AWAY IN THE BASEMENT OR STOW THEM OUT OF REACH ON A CLOSET SHELF?

Considering the sentimental nature of heirlooms, the bulkiness of stuffed animals, and the awkwardness of kindergarten macaroni art, memorabilia can be tricky to deal with for a number of reasons. In this chapter, we'll help you decide how to organize and store your memorabilia so it can inspire you and enrich your scrapbook pages, your home, and your life.

Here's a look at the process of incorporating memorabilia into your scrapbooks and into your organized and inspired space:

① Determine what role your memorabilia should play
② Decide on an organizing method
③ Organize and pare down
④ Store and display your memorabilia

❶ DETERMINE WHAT ROLE YOUR MEMORABILIA SHOULD PLAY

Each piece of memorabilia can serve one or several purposes. You may choose to include certain pieces of memorabilia in your scrapbooks, either as embellishments or as the focal point of a page or album. You might even create a scrapbook filled with nothing but memorabilia. Some items you may choose to store or display in your home, and other items you may prefer to box up and put away. Regardless, it's important to decide how memorabilia will live in your scrapbooks.

❷ DECIDE ON AN ORGANIZING METHOD

Storing your memorabilia effectively will help you integrate your favorite objects into your scrapbooks (and your life). Try some of our favorite methods for organizing our memorabilia:

General organization for long-term storage. If you find you're uncomfortable reading this chapter, you may not be at a place where sorting through your memorabilia feels feasible. That's okay. By all means, honor your feelings. You can still add a greater level of organization to your memorabilia by going through your boxes and labeling them with broad categories, such as "childhood," "high school," "college," etc. This step alone will make it easier to find particular items if you decide to include them on a scrapbook page or display them in your home. Once you've labeled your boxes, create a list of items or categories of items you have.

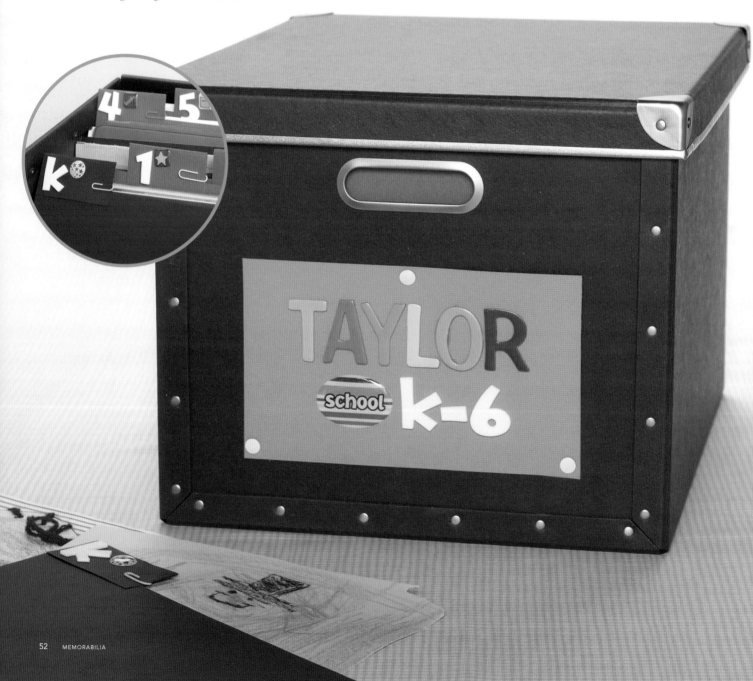

Mimic your photo-organizing system. For the memorabilia pieces you'd like to use on your scrapbook pages, the simplest approach is to categorize them using the same system or systems you use for your photographs. This is great news, right? One less decision to make! Whether you organize your photos chronologically or by topic, if you mimic this system for your memorabilia, you'll be more likely to have the right item handy when you're ready to use it.

Rotating system. For memorabilia you would rather display around your home than use in your scrapbooks, a rotating system will help you enjoy more of your memorabilia collection. Here's how it works: First, decide on a rotation schedule such as seasonal, monthly, or random (whenever you feel like it). Then gather the memorabilia into groups based on how you'd like to display them. If you decide to rotate memorabilia seasonally, create 4 groups (one for each season). For monthly rotations, create 12 groups (one for each month). For a random rotation, decide first where the items will be displayed, and then create groupings of items that fit together in a display.

❸ ORGANIZE AND PARE DOWN

Collect your memorabilia from its current storage location and sort it based on your selected organizing scheme. Here are some pointers to help you cut down:

Think about what memorabilia is important to you before going into the depths of your deepest closet. We know it can get really tricky to decide what to keep and what to send off to a happier home. Every piece of artwork your child created with his two tiny hands seems like a masterpiece. (We can totally relate since we have seven budding artists between us!)

An item has more meaning to you when you understand what it represents in your life. You don't need to keep every object that symbolizes the same experience, timeframe, or relationship in your life. And feel free to let go of things that aren't important to you. If you don't remember where you got it or who gave it to you, let it go. Freeing yourself from excess memorabilia will allow you to truly enjoy the pieces you do keep.

BASIC TIPS TO KEEP YOUR COLLECTIONS SAFE

- Keep your favorite keepsakes accessible and easy to enjoy. If you don't, what's the point in keeping them?

- Protect your mementos by storing them in a cool, dry location, out of sunlight. Avoid your basement whenever possible.

- Invest in a fire-resistant safe to keep valuable mementos and keepsakes protected.

- Protect breakables by wrapping fragile items in tissue paper or bubble wrap before storing.

- Make color copies on acid-free paper of important newspaper articles and clippings you'd like to preserve.

- Use acid-free spray to preserve paper items that contain acid.

❹ STORE AND DISPLAY YOUR MEMORABILIA

Once you decide to keep a piece of memorabilia for your scrapbooks, you'll want to remember you have it when it comes time to create a related page or project. Likewise, if you're holding on to a bulky, non-scrapbookable item because it's meaningful to you, you'll want to store it in a way that allows you to enjoy it. That's where smart storage comes in. To keep your memorabilia accessible, consider using some of our favorite storage solutions:

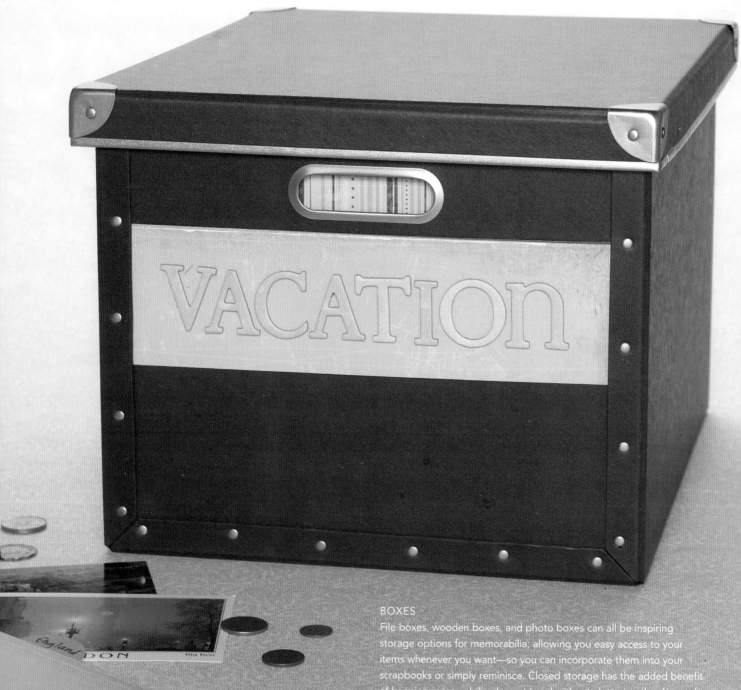

BOXES
File boxes, wooden boxes, and photo boxes can all be inspiring storage options for memorabilia, allowing you easy access to your items whenever you want—so you can incorporate them into your scrapbooks or simply reminisce. Closed storage has the added benefit of keeping memorabilia close at hand without cluttering the décor of your home with outdated or incongruous items.

GLASS JARS

For items you want to enjoy on a daily basis, consider the contained visibility that comes with storing items in glass jars. This solution allows meaningful items that inspire your scrapbooking to accent your room's décor.

BASKETS

Storing special letters and keepsakes in a basket allows you to keep these mementos neatly contained and easy to access at the same time. To add a personalized flair to a storage basket, embellish the front with a fun, inspiring label.

RUSH HOUR-IRELAND

travel

LOUVRE

memories

CLIPBOARD DISPLAY

Use oversized clipboards to display postcards and ticket stubs from recent travels. Or consider using this idea to display kids' artwork. This is the perfect place to employ a rotational display so you can keep your most recent—or most memorable—memorabilia items in view. For other display-worthy items, try the following:

• A shadow box to display postcards, matchbooks, and photos from a favorite vacation or recent holiday

• A bulletin board to create a casual and easily changeable display

• Shelves, frames, or small magnetic boards to house dimensional memorabilia

NOW WHAT?

We've covered the basics of making memorabilia an organized and inspired component of your scrapbooks—and now it's time to take action. Take the quiz on the next page to determine what role memorabilia will play in your scrapbooks, workspace, and home.

CHAPTER ⑤ QUIZ

MEMORABILIA

① What types of memorabilia do you have?

- ☐ Trophies/awards
- ☐ Certificates
- ☐ Letters, cards, postcards
- ☐ Ticket stubs, programs, newspaper clippings
- ☐ Quilts, afghans, handkerchiefs, doilies
- ☐ Glass and porcelain items
- ☐ Knick knacks
- ☐ Clothing: wedding dresses, prom dresses, baby clothes
- ☐ Toys and stuffed animals
- ☐ Objects like watches, cameras, pocket knives, etc.

② Where is it currently stored?

....

....

....

③ How important is your memorabilia to you?

- ☐ Extremely important
- ☐ Very important
- ☐ Somewhat important
- ☐ Unimportant

④ Do you enjoy your memorabilia—either by going through it, seeing it, or displaying it—on a regular basis?

....

....

....

....

⑤ Do you or would you like to use your memorabilia in your scrapbooks?
☐ Yes ☐ No

⑥ Are you able to find your memorabilia to incorporate into your scrapbook pages when you want it?
☐ Yes ☐ No

RECAP

The degree of importance memorabilia has to you should dictate its prominence or placement in your home. If you listed memorabilia as extremely important yet you keep it in a box in storage in your home (attic, basement, garage, etc.), things are out of sync. Consider using one of the storage and display solutions discussed in the chapter to bring these items out of hiding and into your life so you can enjoy them.

If you want to use your memorabilia on your scrapbook pages but aren't able to find it when you want it, try one of the memorabilia organizing methods presented in the chapter.

If you'd like to enjoy your memorabilia but don't want it on display in your home and you don't like to include it in your regular scrapbooks, create a scrapbook just for your memorabilia and use pictures of dimensional or bulky items that won't fit in the book.

CHECKLIST

- Create your vision…what role will memorabilia play for you?

  ☐ Use in scrapbooks

  ☐ Create a scrapbook of just memorabilia

  ☐ Display in home

  ☐ Put in long-term storage

- Decide on an organizing scheme.

  ☐ Same as photos:

    ☐ Chronological

    ☐ By topic

  ☐ Rotating system

  ☐ Broad organization

- Organize and pare down.

  ☐ Keep the memorabilia that has the most meaning to you

  ☐ Let go of things that are no longer important to you

  ☐ If you have many things that effectively represent the same memory, person, or time, select those that are most meaningful to you to keep

- Store and display.

  ☐ Store memorabilia as an embellishment on your scrapbook pages

  ☐ Display

    ☐ Shadow box

    ☐ Oversized clipboard

    ☐ Acrylic box frame

    ☐ Bulletin board

    ☐ Memorabilia shelf

    ☐ Small magnetic board

  ☐ Books

  ☐ Boxes

  ☐ Other _____

ORGANIZED
& INSPIRED

Stories

REMEMBER WHEN YOUR SON HIT HIS FIRST HOME RUN OR HOW IT FELT TO HOLD YOUR
NEWBORN DAUGHTER FOR THE FIRST TIME? STORIES LIKE THESE PLAY A VITAL ROLE IN YOUR
SCRAPBOOKS. SOMETIMES THEY FILL IN DETAILS THAT ARE MISSING FROM YOUR PHOTOS.
OTHER TIMES THEY SERVE AS THE INITIAL SPARK TO INSPIRE A LAYOUT.

In this chapter, we'll help you discover how
to capture thoughts and ideas, create inspired
journaling, and save your stories in ways that allow
you to incorporate them into your scrapbook pages.

Here's a look at the process of incorporating
stories into your scrapbooks and into your
organized and inspired workspace:

① Determine which stories you want to tell
② Select an organizing method
③ Organize and pare down
④ Capture and store your stories

❶ DETERMINE WHICH STORIES YOU WANT TO TELL

From capturing the who, what, when, where, and
why of an event to sharing a delightful personality
trait of a loved one—your life is ripe with stories
waiting to be told. You just need to decide what
types of stories you want to record and when and
how you're going to save them. Then be on the
lookout for inspiration.

Keep in mind that you'll be much more likely
to save interesting thoughts and impressions if
you keep a pen and paper handy. Try carrying a
notebook in your purse, keeping a journal on your
nightstand, or stashing note cards inside your camera
bag—or a combination of the three. Another idea is
to literally "record" your story ideas by calling your
answering machine or using a voice recorder.

If you prefer to type your stories, set up
journaling files on your computer, organized by
date or by topic. Or start a blog (private or public,
it's up to you). It can be a fun means of sharing
information, and your chronological entries can
serve as a reference for future scrapbooking projects.

Visit Wendy's blog at wendysmedley.typepad.com
and Aby's blog at creativeorganizing.typepad.com!

❷ SELECT AN ORGANIZING METHOD

Once you have a collection of stories waiting to join your scrapbooks, it's important to organize them in a way that will help you use them later. The following organizational solutions, which happen to be some of our favorites, may be right for your stories too:

Chronological organization. This system involves sorting your stories chronologically, either based on event dates or the time when a story comes to you. Stories you write in a notebook about your daily life will be naturally chronological. If you want to organize random memories chronologically, set up a file on your computer so you can insert new memories wherever they fit. Or write thoughts or memories on cards and store them in a file box or folder. This can work well for any journaling you want to include along with your chronologically organized photos.

Random organization. If gathering all of your stories in one place is more important to you than actually sorting them based on a specific system, it's okay to do just that. Bring all your journaling ideas together—and don't forget to label what you've got so your stories can find their way onto your scrapbook pages.

Categorical organization. For stories that are connected to people and places as opposed to specific dates or seasons, categorical organization makes more sense. Try organizing your journaling ideas into the same categories you use for your photos (by individual child, relationship stories, stories about the whole family, etc.).

❸ ORGANIZE AND PARE DOWN

After you've settled on an organizing method that works for your stories, you're ready to get sorting. While you probably won't need (or want) to cut down the number of stories you save, you may want to separate out the stories you plan to use on scrapbook projects and store them with your scrapping supplies. Other stories can be saved elsewhere in journals.

❹ CAPTURE AND STORE YOUR STORIES

After you've organized your stories and you're ready to put them away or put them on display, give one of these options a try:

ALTERED CLIPBOARD

Hang a personalized clipboard in a central area of your home (kitchen, hallway, laundry room) to help you capture story ideas and family quotes on the fly. Since ideas and insights can come to you at any time, having a story-capturing tool nearby will come in handy more often than you realize.

WRITER'S NOTEBOOKS

Create a writer's notebook or two that you can keep
handy in your purse, in your camera bag, or on your
bedside table. Use a notebook that fits your style
and needs, whether it's an elegant bound journal or
a loose-leaf binder.

CARD FILES, DRAWERS, AND BOXES

Box storage—including card files, drawers, and boxes—is a great way to store journaling ideas or to create a cross-reference system for stories kept elsewhere, such as your computer or journal. Acid-free cards can be removed from the card file system and stored with photos and other scrapbook materials once you are ready to work on a project. (You can even use the actual card directly on your page!) And of course, you can embellish your storage box to make it fit your space.

ELECTRONIC STORAGE

If it's easier for you to write with a keyboard than with paper and pen, store your stories and journaling ideas electronically. Whether your photos are digital or printed, your journaling can stay on your computer until you're ready to add it to a scrapbook page. If a story corresponds with certain digital photos, simply include your story document in the same electronic file folder as the corresponding photos. If a story corresponds with photo prints, try printing your story and storing it with your photos or jot down the story's location on a card paired with your photos.

NOW WHAT?

We've covered the basics of making stories an organized and inspired component of your scrapbooks—and now it's time to take action. Take the quiz on the next page to help you decide what role stories should play in your scrapbooking.

TIP Here are some journaling ideas to help you get started:

- Use lists, quizzes, or other journaling prompts found in idea books and magazines to unlock your stories.

- Ask family members what's important to them or what they recall about an event or particular phase of their lives.

- Collect your family's favorite quotes and silly phrases to form the basis of a scrapbook story or an entire album.

CHAPTER 6 QUIZ

STORIES

① Think about the stories you've already told in your scrapbooks. Which are your favorites? Which did you enjoy telling the most?

----

② Brainstorm a list of stories that you would still like to tell—what are the things you want to record?

----

③ Look back at questions 1 and 2. How do you like to tell your stories? Do you prefer complete narratives? Funny quotes or snippets? Lists?

----

④ When do you feel inspired to write?

☐ When you first think of an idea, wherever you are

☐ After you've had time to reflect on an idea for a while

☐ In the morning, afternoon, or evening

⑤ What conditions make it easiest for you to write out your thoughts? Check all that apply.

☐ In quiet and solitude

☐ Among activity and interaction with others

☐ In proximity to my computer or laptop

☐ With my journals or writer's notebooks nearby

☐ With music in the background

☐ At a comfortable desk and chair

☐ In a comfortable chair or bedside writing station with notebooks, journals, and pens

☐ At a park, coffee shop, or other location away from home

⑥ How do you like to record your stories? Is it easier to jot down a note on the go, so you don't forget an idea, and then go back to it and write it up later, or do you need to write everything out when the inspiration strikes?

----

⑦ When you have a story written down, does it help you to store it with your photos or do you prefer to keep them separated?

RECAP

Thinking about the reasons you write helps to clarify what works and what doesn't work for you as a writer. Writing can be tricky enough as is—no need to force yourself to write the "right" way when it's really about letting yourself be inspired and being prepared to capture that inspiration before it leaves!

There are two things that can complicate writing: when and where. Use your answers to questions 4 and 5 to recognize your ideal writing conditions. If you like to write in the morning, on the computer, with activities around you, you could keep your laptop in the kitchen. Pack the kids' lunches the night before so you can quickly write up your morning's inspiration while the kids eat their cereal.

Prefer to write by hand? Substitute an altered clipboard for the laptop and you're good to go.

Or, if you need a tranquil space to write in, take your writer's notebook and head for the family room in the afternoon when the baby is down for a nap. Put on your favorite music and let the ideas flow!

Once you've found a where and a when that work for you, think about how you'd like to organize and store your stories once they're written.

CHECKLIST

- Decide what stories or types of stories you would like to tell.
- Choose things you want to change to make your writing process more effective.
- Carve out time to write.
- Decide on organizational strategies for your stories.
  - ☐ Chronological
  - ☐ Categorical
- Implement solutions to help you capture your stories.
  - ☐ Altered clipboard
  - ☐ Writer's notebook
  - ☐ Computer files or blog
  - ☐ Other _____
- Choose which storage solutions you will use to store your stories and story ideas.
  - ☐ File away in card files, drawers, and boxes
  - ☐ Keep them in my writer's notebook
  - ☐ Store in my photo storage system
  - ☐ Store electronically
  - ☐ Other_____

ORGANIZED
& INSPIRED

Products

WE KNOW HOW EASY IT IS TO GET SUCKED INTO A SCRAPBOOK STORE BY ALL THE BEAUTIFUL PAPERS, RIBBONS, CHIPBOARD, AND RUB-ONS. WITH AN ENDLESS ARRAY OF NEW SCRAPBOOK PRODUCTS ON THE MARKET, NOT TO MENTION WHAT'S IN YOUR STASH AT HOME, IT'S EASY TO GET LOST IN THE POSSIBILITIES, LOST IN THE MOMENT, AND (SOMETIMES) JUST PLAIN LOST. IF YOU'RE BURIED UNDER A SEA OF WELL-INTENTIONED SCRAPBOOK PURCHASES, YOU KNOW WHAT WE'RE TALKING ABOUT.

In this chapter, we'll help you let go of the product that isn't serving you well and show you how to surround yourself with supplies that empower you in your pursuit of meaningful layouts. We'll also share some of our favorite options for storing and organizing all that stuff.

Here's a look at how to take control of the scrapbook supplies in your soon-to-be organized and inspired space:

①Determine what's working and what's not
②Select an organizing method
③Organize and pare down
④Store and display your products

❶ DETERMINE WHAT'S WORKING AND WHAT'S NOT

Before you decide to reorganize every last inch of your product stash, scan through it and determine which products are helping you accomplish your scrapbooking mission and which are just taking up space. While you're at it, keep an eye out for organizational methods that are already enhancing your scrapbooking process. You don't want to rework a system that's working just for the sake of making a change.

❷ SELECT AN ORGANIZING METHOD

Build on the good things you've already got going—and consider some of these options to take care of the products that aren't organized in ways that suit your creative process:

Organize by color. To implement this organizing method, group items together based on their color, as opposed to their function. For example, keeping all your pink embellishments together—buttons, ribbon, brads, and stickers—in a single container will make it a snap to find exactly the right trimmings for a page that needs a touch of pink.

Organize by activity. This method involves sorting your supplies by item type and function. For example, you could group together all your stamping supplies (such as ink pads, cleaners, acrylic blocks, and stamps).

Organize by manufacturer or product line. If you think of your products in terms of who made them, consider storing everything based on manufacturer name or product line. With this strategy you can sort products by type and then by manufacturer or product line. Or you can store a variety of products (papers, letter stickers, ribbons, embellishments) from a single manufacturer in a single storage container.

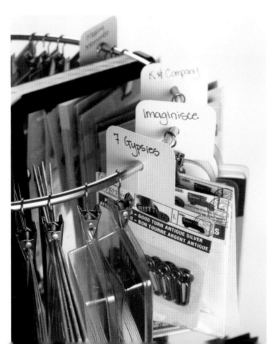

Organize by topic. Sorting (and ultimately storing) your products by topic makes it easy to pull out the right paper and embellishments when you're working on a themed album or project. Topics to consider include seasons (grouping items by spring, summer, winter, and fall), birthday, travel, specific holidays, and baby. Select categories relevant to your stash and your projects.

Organize by project. What about grouping together all the products you need for specific scrapbook projects? With this organizing method, you pull together all the items you need for a project—including the cardstock, photos, tools, accents, and everything in between—and store it in a portable container.

❸ ORGANIZE AND PARE DOWN

Once you've selected your organizing method, it's time to dig in and start sorting. Filter out existing supplies and products that don't meet your needs. Your goal is to keep (and buy) only those products you truly love—those that will actually be useful in your scrapbooking process. Don't be afraid to give away supplies that are outdated and you know you'll never use. Let go of what's not working for you.

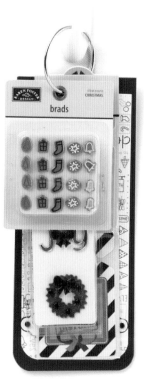

❹ STORE AND DISPLAY YOUR PRODUCTS

When selecting storage solutions, keep in mind products that need to be both visible and portable. Maybe one or two of our favorite ideas will work for you:

HOOKS

Group smaller items together on jump rings and then hang them from hooks in your space. This storage solution can be tucked neatly behind closed cabinet doors. Just swing the door open, and at a glance, you can easily see your products.

ALTERED TRAYS

A decoupaged wooden tray is perfect for storage on a shelf or in a storage cube. Using an altered tray allows you to bring a touch of color and style into your scrapbook space using some of your most inspiring supplies. Add an extra storage component to your tray with cups that can hold smaller items.

flat
sticker letters

sticker letters

3D letters

GLASS JARS

From ribbon, to buttons, to rubber stamps, if you need to see your product to be inspired by it, it's hard to beat a glass jar. To store and display diverse supplies, use jars of varying sizes and shapes in your space.

LIDDED BOXES

Boxes can house a variety of scrapbooking products, keeping them within reach but out of view. Adding lids to your box storage brings the extra benefit of protection from dust and light.

NOW WHAT?

We've covered the basics of making product an organized and inspired component of your scrapbooks—and now it's time to take action. Take the quiz on the next page to figure out how to make your products work for you.

CHAPTER (7) QUIZ

PRODUCTS

① Which products in your stash do you find uninspiring, cumbersome, or not in line with your reasons for scrapbooking?

....

....

....

② Which products in your stash are you holding onto out of guilt? (If you look at it and think, "I paid good money for this, I may need it some day, it was a gift, or it's wasteful not to use this," you're probably keeping it out of guilt.)

....

....

....

③ Which products make you want to create?

....

....

....

④ List the products that you need to reorganize (the ones that are hard to find or that you keep forgetting you have).

....

....

....

....

⑤ List which products are well organized for you (always easy to find, simple to know what you have).

....

....

....

....

⑥ Which storage solutions are working best for you? Write down products that are stored in ways that make them easy to retrieve and put away.

....

....

⑦ What types of storage containers are you using that work well for you? (Use your answers to question 6.)

☐ Open

☐ Closed

☐ Product is visible

☐ Product is not visible

☐ Portable

☐ Stationary

⑧ What types of storage containers are you using that don't work well for you?

☐ Open

☐ Closed

☐ Product is visible

☐ Product is not visible

☐ Portable

☐ Stationary

RECAP

Go back to your answers for questions 1 through 3. What are they telling you? Do you tend to keep only things you love—items that inspire your creativity? Or, through the years, have you held onto products that no longer fit your vision for scrapbooking? Give yourself permission to let go of things that you really won't use and free up some room, both physically and mentally, to focus on the things that really get you excited to scrapbook.

And next time you're at the scrapbook store, keep this chapter in mind. It's better to buy a little of something that you truly love than a lot of something that's on sale but doesn't fit your style or feed your creativity. You'll just end up giving it away later anyway.

Finally, think about the other storage solutions you've chosen as you've gone through previous chapters of the book. What can they tell you about how you'd like to organize and store your products? If you've come to the conclusion that you're inspired to scrapbook by seeing your products but you keep them in little cardboard boxes on the highest shelf in the closet, you might want to rethink your storage options!

Remember, it may make sense to use multiple organizing methods, even within the same product family. And nothing is locked in stone! You can always change your mind later.

CHECKLIST

- Create your vision: take stock of your current products and organizational methods and determine what's working.

- Select organizing methods: use your answers to the quiz in this chapter and in chapter 3 to select organizing methods for your products.

- Next to each organizing method, list which products you'll organize in this way.

  ☐ Organize by activity _____

  ☐ Organize by topic _____

  ☐ Organize by manufacturer or product line _____

  ☐ Organize by color _____

  ☐ Organize by project _____

- Organize and pare down: sort through your stash and let go of products that you don't use, need, or love and those that you're holding onto out of guilt! Keep products that inspire you to create.

- Decide on storage solutions for the inspiring supplies you have left.

  ☐ Hooks

  ☐ Altered trays on shelves

  ☐ Glass jars

  ☐ Lidded boxes

  ☐ Other _____

ORGANIZED
& INSPIRED

Tools

TOOLS AREN'T EXACTLY THE EYE CANDY OF A SCRAPBOOKING SPACE. IN FACT, BULKY
SCANNERS, ODDLY COLORED PAPER TRIMMERS, AND BIG PRINTERS CAN BE TOUGH TO
INCORPORATE INTO A BEAUTIFUL, COORDINATED SPACE. BUT ORGANIZING AND STORING
YOUR TOOLS WISELY CAN HELP YOU FIND THE HAPPY BALANCE BETWEEN FUNCTIONAL
AND INSPIRATIONAL.

Your tools are the non-consumable, reusable
items you use to create a scrapbook, including
your camera, trimmer, cutting mat, computer,
printer, scanner, scissors, stamps, punches, rulers,
and more. The purpose of these tools ranges from
performing very basic and essential functions (e.g.,
taking photos or cutting photo mats) to saving you
time and creative hassle (e.g., using a circle punch
in place of a tracing template and scissors).

In this chapter, we'll share effective ways to
organize and store your tools, and we'll help you
prioritize your storage options by separating your
essential tools from those that are less important.

Here's how to make your tools an integral
part of your almost-completely organized and
inspired space:

① Decide how you want to use your tools
② Select an organizing method
③ Organize and pare down
④ Store and display your tools

❶ DECIDE HOW YOU WANT TO USE YOUR TOOLS

While they may not be the most inspiring items
in your space, tools are key to helping you
streamline your creative process. When deciding
how you want to organize and store your tools, it's
important to have an underlying vision to guide
your actions. Decide now what's important in
terms of convenience and accessibility—and move
forward with an understanding of what each tool
actually contributes to your scrapbooking process.

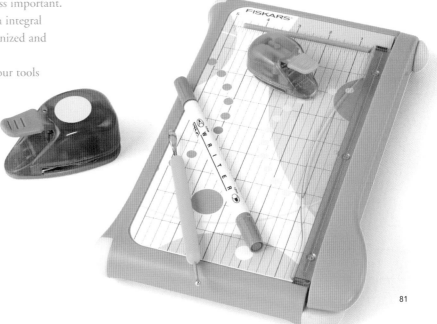

② SELECT AN ORGANIZING METHOD

Consider these organization approaches for your scrapbooking tools:

Tools with consumables. One option is to group your tools and their associated consumables together. For example, essential stamps could be organized with your inks, stamp cleaner, and cleaning pad. Paper piercers and foam mats could be stored with your brads and eyelets. All of your journaling supplies (tools, pens, paper, and more) could be grouped in one place.

Rotating system. With a rotating organizing system, you move tools into your primary work area on a project-by-project or seasonal basis. Group your tools into categories that make sense to you based on projects and seasons. For example, your flower stamps may become essentials while you're working on a springtime page or a mini-album about your garden.

Essential vs. unessential. Essential tools are those you use for nearly every project, and unessential tools are those you use only occasionally. Distinguishing between the two types of tools in your organizing scheme helps you prioritize where to store them in your overall workspace. Keeping your essentials in one place and your non-essentials in another can help you create a working space that's friendly and productive. For example, if you use computer journaling on every layout you create, it makes sense to relocate your computer and printer into your scrap space. Or invest in a laptop.

TIP If it's hard to decide which items are essential to your scrapbooking process, sit down and make a layout right now (seriously, right now!) so you can better understand which tools you use regularly.

❸ ORGANIZE AND PARE DOWN

Once you've decided how you'd like to organize your tools, it's time to start sorting! Like all other scrapbooking essentials, the more you can narrow down the tools you use and love, the easier it will be to find, access, and maintain your organizing system in the future.

❹ STORE AND DISPLAY YOUR TOOLS

After you determine which tools are essential, the next step is storing them accessibly. Here are a few of our favorite ways to store our tools:

TRAY/LAZY SUSAN

This form of open storage keeps all of your essentials together and within reach. With a quick spin, you can see everything you own and easily grab the tool you need.

DRAWERS

Drawers are an option for hiding away scrapbooking items (like tools) that aren't terribly inspiring to the eye. Drawers allow you to easily see and access everything inside. Consider adding containers like glass votives, small metal buckets, or drawer organizers to create compartments and keep items separated inside a larger drawer.

CABINETS AND CLOSETS

Closed storage is an option for large, bulky tools such as paper trimmers, scanners, and printers. A cabinet or closet can help you keep these items out of sight when they're not in use.

CROPPING BAG

If you crop at home and away from home, consider investing in an extra set of essential tools that you can keep packed in your cropping bag. For your well-stocked cropping bag, start with our basic tool kit and then add your personal favorite tools and supplies.

NOW WHAT?

We've covered the basics of making tools an organized and inspired component of your scrapbooks—and now it's time to take action. Take the quiz on the next page to explore how you use your tools.

BASIC TOOL KIT

Store your basic tools together in a portable container so you can quickly access them for every project and easily carry them away from your space. This basic tool kit includes:

- Portable paper trimmer
- Small scissors
- Black archival pen for journaling
- Pencil
- Pencil sharpener
- Art gum eraser
- Paper adhesive
- Photo adhesive
- Portable container to store all of the above tools

You can use this list or create one more tailored to your process.

CHAPTER (8) QUIZ

TOOLS

If you aren't sure of your answers to the questions below, scrapbook a few pages and pay attention to the tools you use for every page. Or look through some of your most recent layouts and projects to see which tools you used the most.

① What do you consider to be your essential tools? List the tools you use every time or nearly every time you scrapbook.

....
....
....
....

② Are there tools that you don't use as much but that you still enjoy? List these less-essential tools.

....
....
....
....

③ Now take a look at the rest of your tools. Be honest—which ones should you kick to the curb because you haven't used them in years?

....
....
....

④ Are there any tools that are large, bulky, or unattractive that you'd like to hide away? Which ones?

....
....

⑤ Do you prefer your favorite tools to be visible and within reach when you're working, or do you prefer a clean and uncluttered workspace?

....
....

⑥ Are there any other considerations you need to make in terms of workspace for your tools? For example, are there tools that need to remain out because they're too heavy or cumbersome to hide away?

....
....
....

⑦ Do you own any tools that would be easiest to use at a standing, counter-height work surface? What are they?

....
....
....

RECAP

Tools can be a blessing and a curse to the scrapbooker—we love what they can help us do, but when they overtake our workspace, they can keep us from getting anything done. Use your answers from the quiz to determine which tools you cannot live without, which you only use once in a while, and which you can part with.

Understanding how you use your tools helps you to come up with an effective way to organize and store them. For example, if you use your scissors, adhesive, and ruler on every layout you make, keep them together in an easy-to-access bin on the top of your workspace. The next time you sit down to scrapbook, you'll have your essentials ready to go!

CHECKLIST

- Use the answers you've recorded in past chapters to help you make decisions about appropriate storage containers and locations for your tools. Remember, storage can be

  ☐ Open

  ☐ Closed

  ☐ Visible

  ☐ Not visible

- Decide on an organizing scheme for your tools.

  ☐ Essential and less-essential

  ☐ Rotating system

  ☐ Tools cohabitating with consumables

  ☐ Other

- Organize and pare down by sorting your tools according to your plan and quiz answers.

- Select a storage container for your essential tools that allows them to be easily accessible when you scrapbook. If you have a dedicated workspace, look for a container that you can keep in arms' reach from where you sit when you scrapbook. If you scrapbook at a temporary workspace, look for a portable storage container that allows you to keep your tools easily accessible.

  ☐ Basic tool storage

  ☐ Tray/lazy Susan

  ☐ Another form of open and vertical storage such as a table-top cropping bag

  ☐ Baskets

  ☐ Drawers

  ☐ Basic tool kit basket

  ☐ Cropping bag

- Consider other storage needs and solutions.

  ☐ Cabinets, shelves, and closets

  ☐ Curtains to hide unattractive items

ORGANIZED
& INSPIRED

References

EVEN IF YOU DON'T HAVE A STACK OF SCRAPBOOKING-RELATED PUBLICATIONS, YOU PROBABLY HAVE A REFERENCE LIBRARY OF SOME SORT AT YOUR DISPOSAL. WE'RE TALKING ABOUT THE BOOKS, MAGAZINES, AND MANUALS THAT HELP YOU UNDERSTAND AND IMPLEMENT SCRAPBOOKING FUNDAMENTALS.

Columns from scrapbooking magazines about design or color principles count. Your camera manual counts, as does your favorite book about organization (ahem). These are your go-to resources filled with new techniques and methods for approaching design, color, photography, and all the other components of scrapbooking.

Don't worry about creating a big reference collection. What's important is having materials that will genuinely help you simplify and enhance your scrapbooking. How? By teaching you to better execute your projects and layouts. By helping you through a roadblock or a creative rut. By sharing guiding principles that will eventually become instinctive.

Cathy Zielske, creative director for *Simple Scrapbooks* magazine, believes in learning and absorbing high-level principles because it makes the process more natural. "Reviewing basic principles of design helps you keep developing your skill as a scrapbooker. The more skilled you become, the easier your pages are to put together," she says in her book *Clean and Simple Scrapbooking*.

Not sure how to make your scrapbooking reference materials work for you? Here are a few ideas for incorporating resources into your space—a space that's getting more organized and inspired by the minute, right?

① Assess your current reference library
② Determine what other resources and books you would like to add to your library over time
③ Select an organizing method
④ Store and display your references

❶ ASSESS YOUR CURRENT REFERENCE LIBRARY

Do your books and magazines address the topics you need help with? It's important to be sure you can find the information you need when you need it. For instance, if you often struggle with layout designs, be sure your reference library offers a healthy dose of idea books and inspiring design schemes within easy reach.

❷ DETERMINE WHAT OTHER RESOURCES AND BOOKS YOU WOULD LIKE TO ADD TO YOUR LIBRARY OVER TIME

While you were assessing your current library, did you notice any holes? Think about the parts of the scrapbooking process that are difficult for you—those that would be much smoother if only you knew more about the concepts behind them. And also decide which concepts you want to learn more about. Then add to your reference library based on those needs and desires.

❸ SELECT AN ORGANIZING METHOD

Decide on an organizational system so you can begin categorizing your reference materials in a way that works for you. As you go, make sure your system isn't so complicated that you spend more time organizing your ideas than using them. Here are some of our favorite ways to organize our own reference materials:

Organize by source. Keep all your books together, organized by author or publisher, and keep all your magazines together, organized by periodical title.

Organize by topic. Categorizing by topic—such as photography, design, and color theory—makes it simple to find the specific info you need when you need it. Remove (or copy) pages from your resources and organize them by topic. If you're not too excited about breaking apart your books and magazines, create a color-coding system to organize by topic. For example, use green sticky notes to flag design ideas, pink for color ideas, and blue for photo ideas.

TIP Are you wondering how reference materials are different from inspiration? Well, your references are tools to help you execute your inspiration. For example, you may have an inspiring title idea tacked to your inspiration board, but a reference book that teaches about type can help you understand how to achieve the same look on a layout.

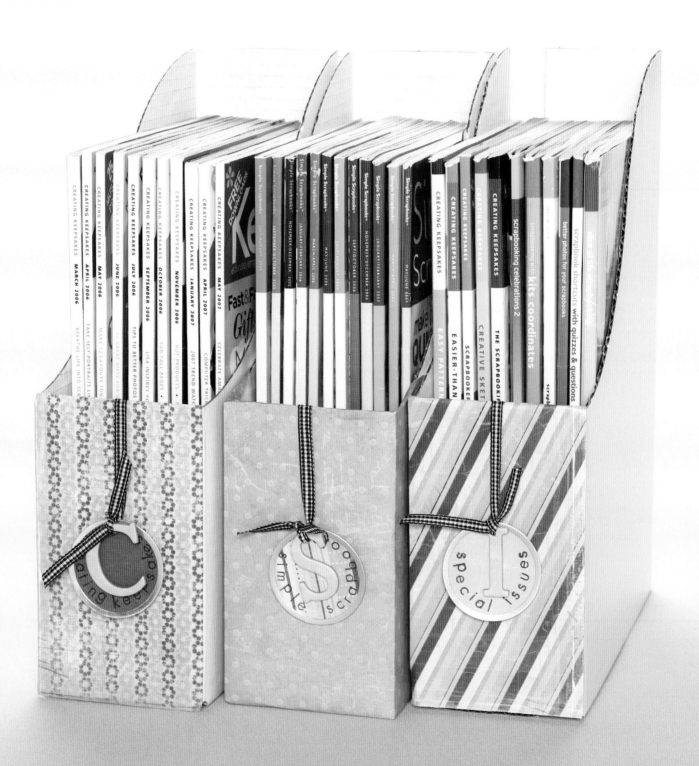

CREATING KEEPSAKES **MARCH 2006**

CREATING KEEPSAKES **APRIL 2006**

CREATING KEEPSAKES **MAY 2006**

CREATING KEEPSAKES **JUNE 2006**

CREATING KEEPSAKES **JULY 2006**

CREATING KEEPSAKES **SEPTEMBER 2006**

CREATING KEEPSAKES **OCTOBER 2006**

CREATING KEEPSAKES **NOVEMBER 2006**

CREATING KEEPSAKES **JANUARY 2007**

CREATING KEEPSAKES **APRIL 2007**

CREATING KEEPSAKES **MAY 2007**

Simple Scrapbooks JULY/AUGUST 2005

Simple Scrapbooks SEPTEMBER/OCTOBER 2005

Simple Scrapbooks NOVEMBER/DECEMBER 2005

Simple Scrapbooks JANUARY/FEBRUARY 2006

Simple Scrapbooks MARCH/APRIL 2006

Simple Scrapbooks MAY/JUNE 2006

Simple Scrapbooks JULY/AUGUST 2006

Simple Scrapbooks SEPT/OCTOBER 2006

Simple Scrapbooks NOVEMBER/DECEMBER 2006

Simple Scrapbooks JANUARY/FEBRUARY 2007

Simple Scrapbooks MARCH/APRIL 2007

Simple Scrapbooks MAY/JUNE 2007

CREATING KEEPSAKES

CREATING KEEPSAKES

CREATING KEEPSAKES

scrapbooking celebrations 2

kits:coordinates

scrapbook shortcuts with quizzes & questions

better photos for your scrapbooks

91

④ STORE AND DISPLAY YOUR REFERENCES

Now that everything's organized, it's time to find suitable containers to hold it all. Here are a few of our favorites:

BOOKSHELF

Since so many reference materials are books or magazines, a bookshelf is a natural choice for storing your reference library. Simply arrange your books on a shelf using your selected organizing method. If possible, keep your reference bookshelf in or near your workspace so they're in reach when you need them.

ELECTRONIC STORAGE

Create an electronic reference library on your computer by saving articles and tips from websites or subscribing to electronic publications that cover topics you'd like to learn more about. Use the same categories to organize your electronic reference materials as you would your paper-based materials.

BINDER

A three-ring binder is a simple, portable storage solution for your reference materials. All you need is a three-hole punch to store loose pages and copies of articles. And if you change your mind, it's easy to remove or rearrange things.

BASKET
If you scrapbook in a temporary space, a basket can make a great portable reference center. Limiting yourself to a single basket will keep the size of your reference library in check, making it easier for you to know what info you have on hand and allowing you to access it easily.

NOW WHAT?
We've covered the basics of making references an organized and inspired component of scrapbooking—and now it's time to take action. Take the quiz on the next page to discover what kind of reference library you would like to build.

CHAPTER (9) QUIZ

REFERENCES

① Which area(s) of scrapbooking is the most challenging for you? (Refer back to the quiz about approach.)

② Do you have an adequate selection of books or other materials in your reference library that cover this topic?
☐ Yes ☐ No

③ Which areas of scrapbooking would you like to learn more about, either because the topic interests you or because it would allow you to scrapbook with less effort?

- ☐ Creativity
- ☐ Photography
- ☐ Writing/journaling
- ☐ Handwriting
- ☐ Design principles
- ☐ Color theory
- ☐ Typography
- ☐ Digital scrapbooking

④ List any books or other resources you would like to add to your library here.

⑤ Are you able to store your reference library where you scrapbook, or would a portable reference library be more helpful?

⑥ How do you feel about tearing out relevant pages from your reference materials?

⑦ Based on your scrapbooking work preferences, which reference library storage solution is most ideal for you?

- ☐ Bookshelf
- ☐ Electronic storage
- ☐ Binder
- ☐ Basket

⑧ Do you find it easier to stay organized with electronic files or paper files? Or are they about the same?

RECAP

Creating a reference library that works for you can help scrapbooking be more fun—if you want to know how to do something, you can easily look it up, learn it, and keep on going!

As you review the quiz, think about what type of library you would like to build. Do you enjoy having complete books that go into greater depth on a topic? Do you like to group your favorite information together in one place, even if that means taking clippings out of a magazine? Or would you rather store your information electronically to free up storage space?

As you decide on a system that works best for your needs, remember that the goal in creating a reference library is to ultimately provide you with the materials, ideas, and tools that will help you realize your own creative vision. The next time you find yourself inspired to play with your digital photos or practice your calligraphy, you'll know right where to go to find some help!

CHECKLIST

- Assess your current reference library.
- Determine what other resources and books you would like to add to your library.
- Organize your reference library.
  - ☐ By source
  - ☐ By topic
- Set up your library.
  - ☐ Purchase or repurpose any necessary storage for your library, such as a bookshelf or other shelving system, binders, baskets, or other portable storage solutions
  - ☐ Set up an electronic reference library (if you want to use digital files)
  - ☐ Create a cross-reference system for your library, if needed

Trying to build up your own reference library? Check out a few of our favorite scrapbooking resources.

Wendy loves:
- *The Big Picture* by Stacy Julian
- *Scrapbooks and Memory Art* by Allison Tyler Jones
- *4,000 Questions for Getting to Know Anyone and Everyone* by Barbara Ann Kipfer
- *Babel* by Jim Houser
- *Yes, It's a Scrapbook!* series by Donna Downey

Aby loves:
- *Clean and Simple Scrapbooking* (and the sequel) by Cathy Zielske
- *Creative Sketches for Scrapbooking* (both volumes) by Becky Higgins
- *Love Your Handwriting* by Heidi Swapp
- *Scrapbook Shortcuts with Quizzes and Questions* (*Simple Scrapbooks* special issue)

SECTION

2

SPACE BY SPACE

Now that we've walked through the pieces of your scrapbooking process, it's time to get to work. We'll help you plan your very own organized and inspired space (using Wendy's space as an example), and we'll help you put it all together (with Aby as your guide). Then, for extra inspiration, we'll show you the breathtaking workspaces of five of our favorite scrapbookers.

PLANNING YOUR SPACE WITH
Wendy Smedley

SCRAPBOOKER AND
CREATIVE EDITOR OF *SIMPLE
SCRAPBOOKS* MAGAZINE

WHAT INSPIRES ME

I want my kids to know how much I love them; I want to tell our
stories; I want to remember the good times and some of the bad.
I want to see where we were so I can appreciate how far we have
come. I want to express my sincere and deep appreciation for
the people I love—and I can do this with my scrapbooks.

COLORFUL PENCILS
LETTER STICKERS
SCRAPBOOK PRODUCTS
CHOCOLATE CHIP COOKIES
BIG TREES
OLD QUILTS
PURPLE PETUNIAS
BLANK JOURNALS
WHITE TEXTURED CARDSTOCK
MY KIDS' ARTWORK

PLANNING YOUR ORGANIZED AND INSPIRED SPACE

with Wendy Smedley

What does your space look like? Do you have an entire room dedicated solely to scrapbooking and other creative pursuits? Do you have a small corner in your home for scrapbooking (yes, even a dining room table!) that you share with other activities and people? As you work toward your own inspired workspace, remember that the most effective type of space is one that melds your scrapbooking approach with your work style, creative preferences, and lifestyle—all while infusing you with a healthy dose of inspiration.

In this chapter, I'll walk you through the process of planning your ideal scrapbooking space—using examples from my space—so you can later set up your inspiring space and start using it!

I just recently reorganized and overhauled my space, following the same process Aby and I teach in this book. I knew I needed a change when I'd find myself sitting on the floor to scrapbook, surrounded by piles of products. And I could never find what I needed. With a large scrapbook room and 8 feet of counter space available, what was the problem? My space just didn't fit "me." Now it's perfect.

❶ UNDERSTAND THE DIFFERENT TYPES OF WORKSPACES

Before we dig into the planning process, it's helpful to understand the different types of scrapbook spaces, their pros and cons, and which may work best for you.

TEMPORARY SPACE

Almost every scrapbooker starts at a temporary workspace, most often the kitchen table. Obviously, this makeshift workspace accommodates non-scrapbooking functions (eating, homework, bills), but when it comes time to scrapbook, you can temporarily pull out your supplies and work for a while before packing everything up again.

While this packing and unpacking can be cumbersome, effective storage solutions can actually make a temporary workspace ideal for many scrapbookers. There is freedom and simplicity that comes with containing your scrapbooking universe in a single rolling case or a plastic box.

Consider this type of workspace if:

• You enjoy socializing when you scrapbook. A temporary space can make it easier to spend time with your family while you scrapbook.

• You're new to scrapbooking and want to try the hobby on for size before investing in a more permanent space.

• You don't have an extra room available that you can claim as your own.

SHARED SPACE

Having a shared space means you have a room in your home dedicated to two or more activities—one of which is scrapbooking. This shared setup offers a more permanent solution than the temporary space because there's no need to haul supplies in and out.

Within a shared space, scrapbooking is just one of the full-time functions of the room. Depending on what else the room is used for, you might have a work surface and open storage solutions always available for your scrapbooking pursuits, or you might need to store your materials in closed containers, keeping everything hidden away when the space is being used by others.

Consider this type of workspace if:

• Having a space that is at least partially dedicated to your hobby makes it easier to include scrapbooking in your daily life.

• You have a home office or similar room that could double as your scrapbooking workspace.

• You don't require complete solitude to enjoy your hobby.

DEDICATED SPACE

A dedicated space is devoted solely to scrapbooking and other creative pursuits, and it generally has only one occupant: the scrapbooker. This arrangement offers a variety of benefits—you can integrate permanent storage into the workspace, keep in-progress pages and supplies out between scrapbooking sessions, and, ultimately, you have the freedom to design every aspect of the space so that it best meets your own scrapbooking needs.

Consider this type of workspace if:

• You have a spare room available in your home or a room that could be converted solely into a scrapbooking room.

• You scrapbook or craft often enough to warrant devoting an entire room to it.

• You enjoy working in solitude.

I definitely scrapbook often enough that it's worth dedicating an entire room to my hobby, but I don't enjoy working in complete solitude. So I created a space that fits these preferences. It's truly a dream come true! My scrapbook room has a door to the kitchen, a door to the living room, a window that looks out into the backyard, and a window that looks into the front yard. I'm completely connected all the time!

❷ CREATE A VISION FOR YOUR SPACE

Wouldn't you love a space that is effective, well-planned, and inspiring all at once? It can be done, and I can show you how. But first, let's define what each of those terms means.

- An **EFFECTIVE** workspace is one that supports your creative process and preferences.

- A **WELL-PLANNED** space offers you easy access to your supplies, which are organized and stored in ways that work for you.

- An **INSPIRING** workspace is filled with items you love and is decorated using fabric, paint, color, and storage containers that inspire you.

As you've guessed, pulling all of these elements together does take time and a focused effort. And you'll find the process works best if you do some up-front planning. Your plan should include a clear vision: how you'd like your space to look, what activities it will accommodate, where you'll store your stuff, and how you'll meld your space with your lifestyle and your creative process. One of the most effective planning tools is a design file—a single place to collect and record all the ideas and information you'll need to create your space.

TIP As you collect things for your design file, dream about your ideal scrapbook workspace. If there were no limitations at all, what would your ideal workspace be like? At this point, don't worry about any limitations, real or perceived.

When I gathered images of creative spaces I liked, I noticed that they had a few things in common—one of which was their use of photographs (displayed both formally and informally) in the room's décor. Since my space had no photographs, I added some that inspire me. I used these clothespins as frames because they allow me to easily swap out my photos.

❸ GET STARTED BY CONSIDERING FOUR KEY DECISIONS FOR YOUR SPACE

- How do you want your space to look?

- What activities will you do in your space?

- What things will you store in your space?

- How can you make your space accommodate your creative process?

As I planned, I realized I wanted to include inspirational items in my space—tangible objects that remind me every day of the reasons I scrapbook. I created a vignette of inspiring items on top of my cabinets so I can easily see it while sitting at my desk. The vignette includes an heirloom typewriter that belonged to my husband's grandfather, a vintage film canister, my favorite photo of my husband, and various other meaningful items.

How do you want your space to look?

An organized and inspired space should be filled with things you love—items that inspire you and remind you why you scrapbook. Begin thinking about what items you could bring into your space to offer inspiration. Create a vision for the color scheme of your space. Ask yourself: What colors make me feel creative? What colors inspire me? At this point, begin pulling together items like paint samples, fabric swatches, and favorite scrapbook products to start defining how your space will look.

Since I draw inspiration from my lettering products and use them on almost every page I create, I store them all in the same area. I hang packages of letter stickers, letter rub-ons, and acrylic letter stamps on my Clip-It-Up display. On the shelves below, I collect bulky lettering products like chipboard letters and wooden letter stamps.

What activities will you do in your space?

During the planning phase, create a clear outline of everything that will be done in your space. Once you have activities in mind, think about the types of furniture you'll need to accommodate the various tasks. You may want a comfortable chair for reading, a writing desk, a computer station, a crafting table, or even an all-in-one work island.

While planning my space, I discovered that I could divide my scrapbooking products into two categories: stuff I use for my work with *Simple Scrapbooks* magazine and stuff I want to keep in my own personal stash. Since I access and use these products differently, I realized it was important to store them separately. And since I often scrapbook using coordinated lines, I decided to store my products in stackable containers organized by manufacturer.

What things will you store in your space?

Keeping in mind the activities you'll be doing in your space, get a feel for your storage requirements. What tools and supplies do you need for each activity? It's easier to stay organized when the items you need for a task are stored in close proximity to where the task is performed. Plan for storage at the outset and evaluate which types of storage best fit how you work. Also, begin thinking about how you'll display your boxes, bins, jars, and other containers—do you need to shop for bookcases, shelving, storage cube systems, or drawer units?

Aside from planning storage space for all your tools, supplies, and photos, make sure you also reserve space to show off your output—finished projects, layouts, and albums.

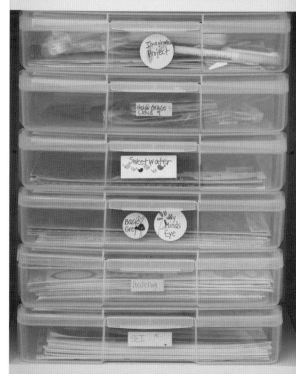

How can you make your space accommodate your creative process?

Remember, the most effective workspace is one that accommodates your approach to scrapbooking and your lifestyle. As you move forward to make your plan:

- Determine which type of scrapbook space will work best for you—temporary, shared, or dedicated.

- Consider the work environment best suited to the different tasks involved in your scrapbooking process, such as writing, page assembly, and so on.

- Decide whether you'll scrapbook more if you can be in a centrally located area in your home that allows you to interact with your family.

- Determine how important it is for you to be able to see your products, tools, and output.

As you plan, keep in mind the flow of materials in and out of your space. Reference materials such as magazines are central to my scrapbook approach (and life!). My magazine rack makes it easy to clip relevant materials and then recycle or donate the rest when I'm finished. What systems can you build into your space to help you maintain order?

I don't necessarily need to see my supplies in order to remember I have them, but I do like to see the new things I have purchased. When planning my space, I decided to include a "new purchase basket" so I can have a dedicated place for the latest additions to my stash.

I like to organize my cardstock by color, and these vertical slots make it so easy for me to flip through and see what I have.

I also considered the outgoing flow of products when planning my space. Since I get a lot of products from manufacturers, I've made it easy to share with others by creating an "extras" giveaway box. This cute solution allows unneeded product to flow out of my space without interrupting my creativity.

NOW WHAT?

We've covered the basics of planning an organized and inspired workspace—and now it's time to take action. Take the quiz on the next page to discover what type of space is right for you.

extras

projects

CHAPTER (10) QUIZ

PLANNING YOUR SPACE

① When you think of your dream scrapbook workspace, what type of space do you envision?
- ☐ Temporary
- ☐ Shared
- ☐ Dedicated

② Take a moment to describe how your dream scrapbook space looks. Include items displayed or used in the space, color scheme, fabrics, and style of furniture and storage accessories.

....
....
....
....
....
....
....

③ Which of these activities need a place in your space?
- ☐ All the steps in your scrapbooking process
- ☐ Writing your story
- ☐ Assembling pages
- ☐ Reading reference materials
- ☐ Sorting and organizing photos and memorabilia
- ☐ Gift wrapping
- ☐ Sewing
- ☐ Knitting
- ☐ Beading
- ☐ Crafts with kids
- ☐ Kids' homework
- ☐ Altering projects
- ☐ Painting
- ☐ Reading
- ☐ Office work
- ☐ Household paperwork/filing
- ☐ Other craft projects
- ☐ Other family/household activities, such as watching TV, playing games, etc.

④ For each activity you marked in question 3, list the items used for that activity. (This will help you determine your storage requirements.)

....
....
....
....
....

⑤ For each activity to be done in your space, write down the type of work environment that is best for you. Consider contact with others, noise, lighting, design elements, etc.

....
....
....

⑥ Jot down ideas that will help your space accommodate your unique creative process. (Refer to prior worksheets and the text in the chapter for ideas.)

....
....
....

RECAP

The space in which you scrapbook can have a great effect on your ability to tap into your own creativity. Discover what type of space works best for you—temporary, shared, or dedicated—and then work to create that space!

Not only will you feel more comfortable scrapbooking in a space designed with your needs in mind, but, if you choose to use the area for other creative projects as well, you may also find yourself inspired to tackle a project left unfinished long ago. And, as we all know, bringing creativity and imagination into your life can lead you to new inspiration for your scrapbooks!

CHECKLIST

- Fill out the quiz to begin creating a vision for your space.

- Create a design file. (See project in back of book.)

- Define the activities you'll do in your creative space.

- Describe the tools and supplies needed to do each of the activities in your creative space.

- Brainstorm ways your space can be set up so that it best accommodates your creative process.

PLAN YOUR SPACE

SCRAPBOOKER
AND ORGANIZING
EXPERT

CREATING YOUR SPACE WITH
Aby Garvey

WHAT INSPIRES ME

Photos tell a story on their own, but there's something magical that happens when you bring together stories and photos on the pages of a scrapbook. It's this ability to tell our stories and share my thoughts, feelings, and love with my family that inspires me to scrapbook.

SCRAPBOOK PRODUCTS
LOVE
THINGS MY KIDS SAY
QUOTES
MOD PODGE
CHANGING SEASONS
MAGAZINES
IDEA BOOKS
CERAMIC BOWLS
TRAYS

CREATING YOUR ORGANIZED AND INSPIRED WORKSPACE with Aby Garvey

Good news! Now that we've talked about the various components of scrapbooking and gone through the planning process, I am here to help you put everything together in your very own organized and inspired workspace. I'll walk you through the basics of setting up your new space—using lots of examples from my own personal scrapbook room. Let's go!

In my space, I have a desk and a creative workstation, so I can work on business projects in the same place where I brainstorm and create scrapbook layouts. On the wall behind my desk hangs what I call a victory board, where I display mementos representing some of my successes. Another board, on the wall facing my desk, is what I call a vision board. It's loaded with images of goals I'm currently working on. I think it's a powerful thing to start my day by looking at reminders of what I've accomplished in the past. Then I turn around, put my back to the past, and start creating the future.

❶ FINALIZE YOUR VISION FOR YOUR SPACE

Go over your design file, pages you've flagged in this book, and the beautiful spaces pictured in chapters 10–16 to finalize your vision for your space. Whether you're creating a dedicated scrap room or a cozy nook in your kitchen, get clear about how you want things to look, feel, and function when you're done.

Establish your priorities. If your budget doesn't permit you to do everything you want to do right away, decide what's most important to change now and what can be done in later phases of the project. Then make design and purchasing decisions based on your budget and your vision. Select a paint color, fabrics, containers, storage, and furniture. And finalize your decisions about which organizing methods to use for the various items in your space.

As you finalize your vision, remember that an organized and inspired scrapbooking space accommodates you, your lifestyle, and your unique creative process.

❷ REVIEW YOUR CREATIVE PROCESS

In preparation for the action you're about to take in the next steps, review your quiz responses and the checklists included throughout this book. Pay particular attention to the things you've learned about your own approach to scrapbooking—and the kind of support (in supplies, organization, and storage) your unique process requires.

❸ ORGANIZE AND PARE DOWN

After clarifying your creative process, you're ready to get your hands dirty. It's time to go through all of your scrapbooking stuff and organize it based on your chosen organizing methods. And yes, I mean all of it. The process of organizing works best when you sort everything you have into logical categories and then decide what stays and what goes.

As you make your piles of "keepers" and "toss-outs," ask yourself: Which items help me accomplish the output I want? Which items fit my style? Which items make it easier and more inspiring

for me to accomplish the things I want to achieve in my space?

I know what you're thinking: "I paid good money for that stuff!" or "How can I possibly get rid of something that was given to me as a gift?" This is no time for guilt. You're on your way to creating an inspiring and organized place where you can create scrapbooks. The things that will help you create scrapbooks you love are the only things that should make it back into your space. No matter how much they cost or who gave them to you, scrapbooking components you don't love won't get used.

I know it's tough to let go of scrapbook supplies, but you can do this! You'll be so glad you did when your space is filled with things you truly love.

Although my space is dedicated to my professional work and scrapbooking hobby, I often have a young visitor. Storing art supplies in a blue bucket within my modular shelving unit makes it easy for my daughter to work on craft projects alongside me as I scrapbook.

❹ SHOP FOR YOUR SPACE

Now comes the step you've been eagerly awaiting—shopping for storage solutions (and furniture) and deciding where everything will go in your space. A shopping trip may seem inevitable, but before you head out with a lengthy list in hand, consider your options for repurposing containers and furniture you already have around the house. Do you already own containers that could be redecorated to satisfy some of your storage needs? Do you have a bookcase you could paint to store your gear?

Once you've determined what you already have at home, you can fill in the gaps by purchasing containers and furnishings that support your established organizing methods. When making your shopping list, refer back to the assortment of containers and storage solutions highlighted throughout section 1 and the notes you've made. Remember to consider your creative process and decide which items may require a portable storage solution. Keep in mind which items you want (or need) to see and which you'll need to access quickly and easily.

Since you'll be shopping for containers to hold specific items, consider how each container's contents will appear and how much space the items to be stowed require. This will help you determine the type of container to purchase in terms of size, shape, and translucency. Take measurements of your space and existing storage solutions, such as bookcases and shelving, to ensure your containers and furniture will fit your space. And take along your design file to refer to color swatches.

Everything in my space is meaningful to me. I was very conscious to use things I loved so the room would make me productive, creative, and happy. For instance, my 8-year-old son sewed the polka-dotted pillow that sits on my chair in the corner, and the colorful artwork hanging on one wall is from a special trip I took to New Orleans with a close friend.

I purchased this ladder-style shelf to store (and display) my glass jars and open containers. This storage solution is perfect for my ribbon and small embellishments, making them accessible and decorative at the same time. And I love the splash of color they add to my space.

Small ceramic bowls (which are actually votive holders) sit on a tray on the ladder bookshelf, holding my assorted collection of metal attachments and embellishments. When I started putting together my space, I had fun deciding how I could repurpose containers like these to add a unique sense of style to my scrapbook storage.

The bottom shelf of my ladder holds a decoupaged, three-shelf box—where I keep all my scraps. Believe it or not, those drawers are a little messy (being scraps, and all), but the box's colorful design makes me feel okay about that.

Since I sometimes purchase scrapbook supplies with one of my two children in mind, I organize some of my products by child. Using binders and storage boxes to hold the two groups of supplies, I can easily find what I need for my upcoming kid-related projects.

❺ GET SET UP

Your organized supplies and your empty storage solutions are now ready to come together in your space. To begin, position your primary work area—whether it's a desk or work table—so it offers the best view of your space. Then position the remaining items around it, keeping inspiring objects and containers where you can see them so they're accessible and motivating to you.

Keep your storage solutions for essentials, such as basic tools, close at hand so you can reach them easily as you scrapbook.

Once your primary workstation is set up, you can take it a step further by creating zones, or groups of items used for a particular function, within your space. For example, create a reference zone like mine—loaded with magazines, idea books, your idea binder, a comfortable chair, and a reading light. Carve out a spot for photo sorting with an empty bin for freshly printed photos, journaling cards, and your photo boxes—everything you need to make photo sorting a breeze.

I store my 12 x 12 cardstock vertically on a shelf, and my 8½ x 11 cardstock sits in a basket with thick cardstock dividers separating the colors. This system makes it easy to flip to the color I want. To make things even easier, I have a color swatch book hanging from the basket to help me keep tabs on favorites and color names. I also keep a Bazzill Basics color wheel inside the basket for easy reference. These two tools are a great resource when it comes to color coordination—plus, it's easy to reorder when my cardstock stash gets low.

I love the convenience of storing all my tools in one place. My Crop-in-Style cube system helps me keep essentials like my paper cutter, stamp pads, acrylic blocks, and tag-making supplies stored neatly away—and yet still within arms' reach of my project table.

As a finishing touch for my space, I embellished four clocks and hung them on my wall to help me keep track of what time it is where my clients live. The clocks obviously serve an important purpose, and they add a fun, colorful design element to my space too.

After getting everything sorted, stored, and in place, I had fun adding the finishing touches to my space by creating personalized labels for many of my containers. I used some of my favorite scrapbooking products to make my tags inspiring and fun.

Now that Wendy's shown you how to plan your space and I've given you some tips for creating a space you love, take a look at the inspiring spaces of five scrapbookers we've chosen to spotlight.

❻ FINISHING UP

Finally, no organizing project would be complete without labels. Labels help you remember what goes where and what you have hiding in closed and opaque containers. When you use your favorite scrapbooking supplies to get creative with your labeling, labels add a touch of style and creativity to your space as well.

Allow your space to evolve over time as you discover what's working and what needs tweaking. And be sure to set aside time after you complete a project to tidy up your space as you go along—keeping it organized and inspiring all the time.

NOW WHAT?

We've covered the basics of creating an organized and inspired workspace—and now it's time to take action. Take the quiz on the next page to start pulling your workspace together.

CHAPTER (11) QUIZ

CREATING YOUR SPACE

① As you pull together the information in your design file and notes from the worksheets, what patterns do you see? (For example, do you see any recurring elements, such as an island workstation, open shelving, baskets, glass jars, metal buckets, etc.)

② What color schemes appeal to you?

③ What types of furniture appeal to you?

④ What is your budget for this project?

⑤ What specific changes could you make in your creative space that would have the greatest impact on you?

⑥ What solutions could you make that would make it easier for your scrapbook space to accommodate your lifestyle?

⑦ What containers and furniture do you have at home that can be repurposed for your scrapbook space?

⑧ What items do you need to purchase?

PLANNING SHEET
Using the answers from the quiz, map out your plan to pull your space together.

My selected color scheme for my space is:

List your selected organizing method and storage solutions for each step in your creative process:

Inspiration

Photographs

Memorabilia

Story

Product

Cardstock

Embellishments

Tools

Reference Materials

SHOPPING LIST

List containers and furniture you'd like to buy for your space. Write down any important dimensions, such as the space itself, things to be stored, or existing furniture (such as depth and height of bookshelves), so you're sure your purchases will fit in your space.

PROJECT LIST

List the projects you want to do to pull your space together—projects such as painting your space or furniture to put in it, sewing curtains, projects from this book, etc. Prioritize this list based on your budget and your answers to questions 5 and 6 on the quiz.

CHECKLIST

- Finalize your vision for your space.

  ☐ Pull together info from your design file and notes from this book

  ☐ Decide how your space will look, feel, and function when you're done—establish your priorities

  ☐ Finalize decisions about organizing methods and storage solutions

- Review your creative process.

- Organize and pare down. Ask yourself:

  ☐ Which items help me accomplish what I want?

  ☐ Which items reflect my style?

  ☐ Which items make it easier and inspire me to accomplish what I want to in my space?

- Shop for your space.

  ☐ Shop at home

  ☐ Create a shopping list

  ☐ Go forth and shop!

- Get set up: position your items in your space so you have

  ☐ Inspiring items in sight

  ☐ Essential items in reach

  ☐ Zones—items used for a single task grouped together

- Finish up—be sure to label your storage containers!

CHAPTER 12

SPOTLIGHT ON

Beth Proudfoot

SIMPLE SCRAPBOOKER
WHO USES ONE APPROACH TO
ORGANIZE EVERYTHING

WHAT INSPIRES HER

"I scrapbook to document stories, thoughts, and feelings for myself
and my family. I love this hobby because it allows me to live a
creative life—and to live more consciously aware of my blessings."

COLOR
GOOD DESIGN
MY FAMILY
THOUGHTS AND FEELINGS
READING
ORGANIZATION
COOL PRODUCTS
STORIES
TYPOGRAPHY
PHOTOS
MUSIC

BETH PROUDFOOT
is a teacher at
bigpicturescrapbooking.com.
She loves to share new and
inspiring color combinations
with students. When she's
not scrapbooking, Beth can
be found organizing anything
and everything in her home—
from toys to linen closets to
scrapbooking supplies. She
and her husband, Kevin, and
their three children live in
Lebanon, New Jersey.

SPACIOUS BUT SIMPLE

Beth and her young family recently moved into a larger
home, which gave her a much larger scrapbooking
space. But, according to Beth, a bigger room doesn't
need to equal more stuff. She made a conscious decision
to surround herself with only the things she loves and
uses. She has restricted her actual "supply space" (for
paper, embellishments, alphabets, and ribbon) to a very
small area of her scrapbooking room. She loves having
everything she needs to create a layout or a project right
at her fingertips instead of having it spread out all over
the room in a hundred different drawers and baskets.

"As I spend more and more time in my space, I learn more about it. I'm always reevaluating and readjusting the space to encourage my creativity and enhance my productivity."

ORGANIZING AND STORING BY COLOR

Everything Beth owns is organized by color. Everything. Sorting this way makes sense for her because she thinks and creates by color. She stores her ribbon by color in clear plastic jars. Her cardstock is divided by color and stored in open shelving. Beneath the cardstock, she keeps her alphabet sets organized using plastic trays. (For some colors, she doubles up—grouping red and pink alphabets together on one tray and orange, yellow, and green alphabets together on another.) Then everything else (paint, buttons, brads, flowers, stars, and other embellishments) is stored in clear plastic drawers.

When Beth buys new products, she separates them by color as soon as she gets home and stores them in the appropriate locations. And for those products she takes out of their original packaging, small clear containers and clear plastic bags usually do the trick.

ACCESSIBLE TOOLS

Beth keeps her most-used tools in small baskets, all placed inside a larger basket that sits on her worktable. This way everything she needs is right there—organized and accessible for daily use.

DISPLAYING OUTPUT

Once she's completed a layout or album, Beth loves to display her work in her scrapbooking space. She puts recent layouts on small easels and arranges mini-albums in a large, open basket. Displaying her output like this serves two purposes:

① It provides personalized décor for her workspace

② It shares what she's created with family members and friends who visit the room

KEEPING IT FRESH

Beth regularly evaluates her products, tools, and books so her space contains only what she truly loves and uses. Her rule is this: If she hasn't used something in three to six months (or if she just doesn't foresee using it) the unlucky product moves to two buckets in the basement. Things she knows she doesn't want go into a donation bucket, while items she's not sure about go into her "just in case" bucket. Every few months, Beth goes through her buckets, moving some things into the donation pile.

REFERENCE CORNER

Next to her comfy, oversized chair in the corner of the room, Beth has a magazine rack that is filled with recent issues and special issues of scrapbook magazines. This inspiring, little reference center is constantly changing, with a rotating system similar to what she has set up for her products. Books and magazines that come off the magazine rack are stored in a large bucket down in the basement.

CHAPTER 13

NEW SCRAPBOOKER (BUT LONGTIME CRAFTER) WHO WORKS IN A TEMPORARY SPACE

SPOTLIGHT ON

Kelly Jeppson

WHAT INSPIRES HER

"Sometimes it's the photo; sometimes it's the paper or the product. I'm also inspired by how other people work and put things together. I have a whole album of magazine scraplifts! But ultimately, I love showing my family the pages or albums that I make and hearing them say (even my four-year-old), 'Remember when we did this?'"

VINTAGE FABRIC
ALPHABET LETTERS
COOKING
TEXTURE AND LAYERING
FARMERS' MARKETS
QUOTES AND BOOKS
LITTLE COLLECTIONS
OLD QUILTS

KELLY JEPPSON is fairly new to scrapbooking, but she's been sewing, decorating, crafting, and writing for years. She loves keeping track of the not-so-ordinary moments that take place every day, because those are what memories are made of. She also loves to create beautiful décor pieces for her home out of paper and simple embellishments. She and her husband, Jared, live in Draper, Utah, with their two young children. In her "spare" time, Kelly teaches writing at a local community college and does freelance writing for magazines.

TEMPORARY SPACE, PERMANENT PRODUCTIVITY

Kelly scrapbooks in the kitchen. Without a dedicated scrapbook room in her house, she's gotten inventive with her storage. She keeps supplies for ongoing projects on shelves in the bottom half of her kitchen pantry. The top half is dedicated to food. She stores tools and products she's not currently using in her basement.

DOCKING PHOTOS

With so many photos on hand, Kelly had to pare down to keep her sanity. She sorted through her stash of older, pre-digital photos and used a photo dock to store only those she thought she would really use on layouts. Her photo dock is divided into categories, like "family," "vacations," and "seasons." The rest of her older photos are in storage, in photo boxes, so she can still access them as needed. Kelly's digital photos are organized and saved on her computer so she can easily print the ones she really likes and store them in her photo dock for scrapbooking projects.

"I love to work in the sunlight, and I love to see what I am working on, because solutions present themselves at different times. I also like to be where the action is! Carting my things around works best for me because I have two small kiddos, who also like to be where the action is. I can sneak in a bit of creativity even if they are eating breakfast or making a mess in the adjacent family room. At the same time, I can easily clean up or store my projects if I need the space for something else."

TWO-IN-ONE PANTRY
Kelly has managed to make scrapbooking
supplies and food coexist comfortably
in the same cupboard—thanks to good
organization and tidy storage containers.

PROJECT BASKET
Kelly keeps supplies for her current
projects in a basket she can leave out on
the kitchen table when she's scrapbooking
and then store in the pantry when it's time
to clean up. When she finishes a project,
she rotates the unneeded tools and supplies
out and adds what she needs for her next
creative endeavor.

MANAGING PRIORITIES

To keep from getting overwhelmed by her many projects, Kelly purchased three green baskets to help her prioritize. She stores one in-process project in each basket and doesn't allow herself to start additional projects until she completes something that's already in a basket. This approach helps Kelly focus her creative energy on her top priorities—and it keeps all of her supplies for ongoing projects neatly stored and easily accessible.

BASEMENT STORAGE

When she has a scrapbooking idea in mind, Kelly pays a visit to her basement to gather supplies. With the help of her project basket, she carries it all upstairs to the kitchen table. This setup allows her to store in-progress projects and supplies in the pantry without packing the cupboard to overflowing. That's a definite must, since Kelly's family actually has to eat at the table! She loves her temporary workspace because she can enjoy her hobby while being close to her kids.

"There's a great sense of accomplishment when I can show something I've made. I've always liked to have bulletin boards, good quotes, and fun photos around to look at."

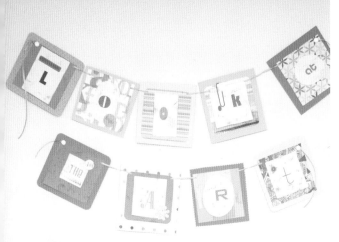

HOME DÉCOR

Take a walk around Kelly's home, and you'll see evidence of her scrapbooking hobby at several turns. She loves to incorporate handmade projects into her home décor. There's framed patterned paper hanging on the wall above her bed and a seasonal layout displayed on the mantle in her family room. A display at the end of her hallway shows off her kids' art projects. Kelly also has a small shelf in her kitchen dedicated to miniature albums and projects she's completed.

CHAPTER 14

SPOTLIGHT ON
Kelli Crowe

PROLIFIC SCRAPBOOKER
WHO SHARES A CRAFT SPACE
WITH HER THREE KIDS

WHAT INSPIRES HER
"I am inspired by everything I see----fashion, color combinations,
clouds, patterns, cartoons, kid art...even laundry. Scrapbooking pulls
together so many of the things I enjoy and organizes it all onto a
nice 12 x 12 piece of paper."

MY CHILDHOOD BACKPACK
FUNNY THINGS MY KIDS SAY
BRIGHT COLORS
PAINT CHIPS AT HOME DEPOT
A BIG SALAD (that someone else made)
CALVIN AND HOBBES COMICS
1980s MUSIC
HOME DÉCOR MAGAZINES
A FRESH STACK OF NOTEBOOK PAPER
CIRCLES

KELLI CROWE is a longtime scrapbooker and crafter who has had her work published in many industry books and magazines. She's also a garden girl at twopeasinabucket.com. Kelli and her husband, John David, live in Alpharetta, Georgia, where she homeschools her three (loud) boys and enjoys Star Trek, Jane Austen books, and photography.

CRAFTING WITH KIDS

Kelli shares her scrapbooking space with her three young sons—who, incidentally, love to experiment with paint, paper, glue, and glitter. Kelli enjoys scrapbooking at the same table where her boys also express their creativity (and she doesn't mind having their crafting supplies within reach for the days when she wants to add beads and finger paint to a layout).

SHARING WITH MESSY HANDS

Kelli purchases and stores all of her materials with messy hands in mind—since she shares her scrapbooking space with three rambunctious boys. The floor is unscratchable, the table's finish lets paint peel off easily, and the oversized sink accommodates playful little hands as they wash out paintbrushes.

"My kids can paint or draw or build at the table while I scrap safely at the counter. There are hand prints and paint splatters all over the place. It's okay—it isn't the dining room."

CLEAR STORAGE

Kelli generally has to see her products to remember to use them, so clear storage is the best solution for her space. She uses glass jars and plastic containers most frequently. And she doesn't really believe in labels because her stock is always changing (and she can already see what's in the containers anyway). While many of her supplies are out where she can see them, she keeps less attractive tools and materials inside her cabinets.

The storage in her space is also designed around the needs of her children. Products her sons can use freely are stored in clear containers within their reach. Materials the boys can use only with supervision (like paints or the stapler) are stored up higher behind cabinet doors.

PORTABLE WORKSTATION

In the evenings, Kelli likes to haul projects and supplies upstairs so she can enjoy her husband's company while also enjoying her hobby. With the help of a fun orange tray, she easily transports items from her downstairs workspace to her upstairs coffee table. She has her circle punch, he has his remote, and everyone is happy.

STORY-SAVING CALENDAR

Capturing stories on the go is a big part of Kelli's scrapbooking process. She takes her camera and calendar everywhere, and she's even trained her family to be on the lookout for ideas. Kelli records quotes, ideas, page sketches, and events in her portable calendar, making it a great reference when she sits down to scrapbook. She keeps past calendars for years in case she ever wants to refer back to a specific date for a project.

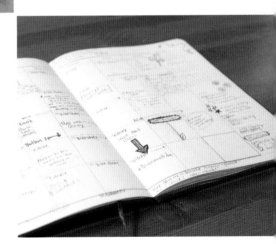

PROJECTS ON DISPLAY

Kelli hangs recent layouts and projects on a big bulletin board in her space, allowing her family members to enjoy her hobby while also adding a dynamic element of décor to the room.

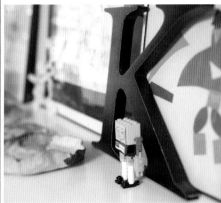

Kelli's sons have as much display space in the room as she does. Their finger-painted masterpieces and imaginative sketches add extra personality to the décor.

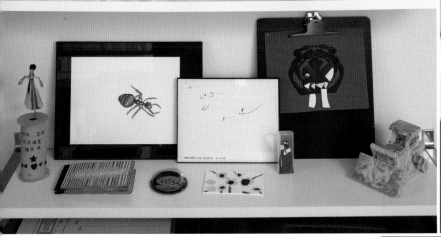

CUT-AND-PASTE IDEA NOTEBOOK

With dozens of ideas popping into her head throughout any given day, Kelli keeps track of her thoughts in four idea notebooks. When something inspires her, she sketches it, takes a photo of it, or cuts it out of a magazine; then she tapes it into one of the notebooks. While their contents are fun and inspiring, Kelli's notebooks are not designed to be pretty. They function as a temporary storage space for her ideas—ideas that inspire about 70 percent of her layouts.

CHAPTER 15

SPOTLIGHT ON

Renee Pearson

DIGITAL AND PAPER
SCRAPBOOKER AND
GRAPHIC DESIGNER

WHAT INSPIRES HER

"Inspiration, for me, is like breathing. It's always there, always around me. I'm constantly taking it all in. Everything I see, smell, and touch inspires me in some way. These things come back to me as I need them. I don't even think about it. It's rare that I can identify a specific inspiration, but I know it all gets mixed into the creative soup."

GINGER PEACH TEA
AMELIE THE MOVIE
AUTUMN
MODERN ART
ARCHITECTURE
LAVENDER BATH SALTS
NICK BANTOCK BOOKS
GREEN
TEXTILES
JAZZ
FURNITURE

RENEE PEARSON was a columnist for *Digital Scrapbooking* magazine. An established name in the digital scrapbooking world, she broke new ground with her best-selling book *Digital Designs for Scrapbooking,* now in its third printing. The sequel to that book was released in spring 2007. Renee and her husband, Kent, make their home in Atlanta, Georgia. They have three grown children.

ZONED FOR CREATIVITY

Renee is not restricted in any way when she scrapbooks. She loves to combine paper and digital elements to record her memories—and she has a workspace that supports anything and everything she wants to do. Her space is divided into different activity zones so she can easily find what she needs for a given project.

CENTRAL WORKSTATION

Renee's worktable island—two cabinet bases beneath a butcher-block top—provides lots of storage. One cabinet holds essential tools: a basic tool kit, a laminator, two guillotine-style paper trimmers, a hole punch, and so on. The second cabinet houses plastic bins, which are filled with inspiration items, memorabilia, genealogy, templates, cards, bookbinding supplies, and more.

"I love my space because it is a perfect reflection of both my taste and my work style. I feel more creative here—and that, for me, is what it's all about."

DIGITAL WORKSPACE

Although Renee's space may look a little minimalist, it's well stocked with the things she needs and loves for scrapbooking. Since she is a digital gal, she doesn't have a lot of the products you'd see in the spaces of scrapbookers who use paper exclusively. To say Renee's two computers (a laptop and a desktop machine) are central to her scrapbooking activities would be an understatement. With the help of her computers, she saves photos to DVD, labels them, and organizes them all in a CD binder. Renee also scans images and stores digital reference materials on CD, organizing them by subject.

PAPER STORAGE

Although Renee has a passion for digital scrapbooking, she still loves her paper products. With the help of clear plastic boxes, she stores paper, buttons, ribbon, and letters by color.

REFERENCE CENTER

The bookcase behind Renee's desk houses her many reference materials. Since she uses a variety of computer programs for her projects, she keeps software manuals on hand for easy access. She also has idea books, design books, and an endless supply of magazines.

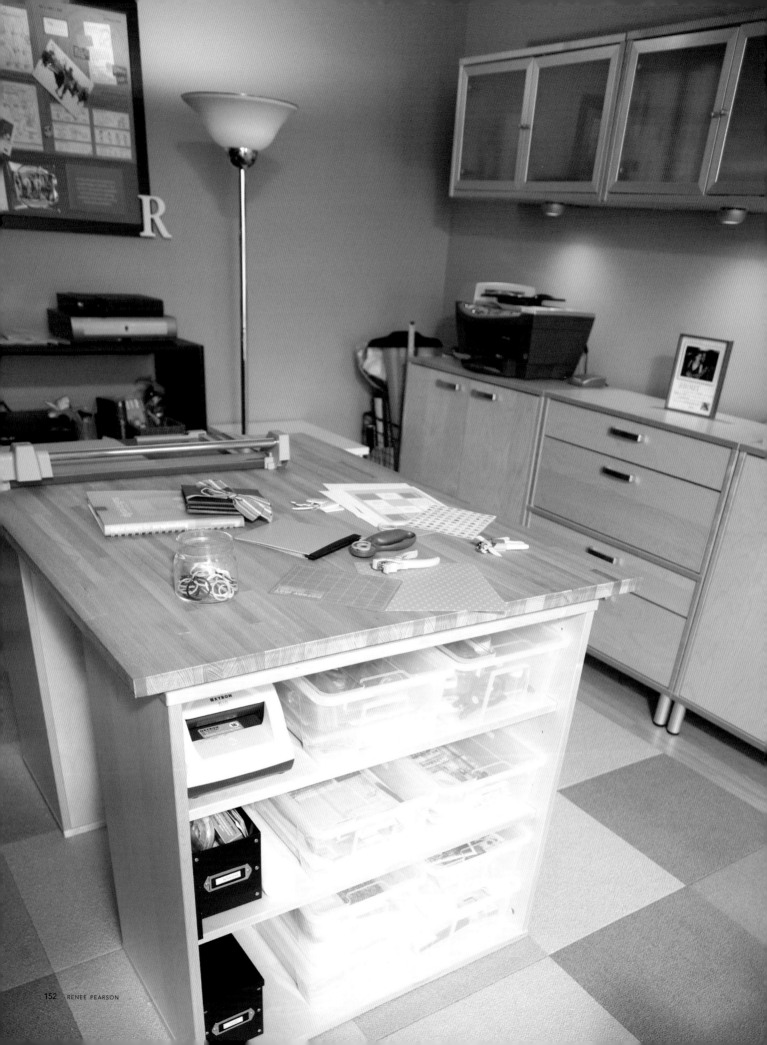

HIDDEN STORAGE
Behind cupboard doors, Renee stores a variety of scrapbook supplies and reference materials. She uses clear containers to hold colorful ribbons, jump rings, and craft flowers that don't fit logically into her other product-organizing systems. Although the containers' contents are visible only when the cupboard doors are open, Renee finds it useful that they are clear because she can easily track down what she's looking for.

WHAT TIME IS IT?
With three different time zones impacting her daily activities, Renee has three clocks in her workspace to keep things straight. The clock on the left represents Stockholm, Sweden, where her son and his family live. The clock in the middle is set to Eastern time (where Renee lives), and the third clock shows West Coast time (where many of Renee's clients are located).

411 BOARD
Above her computer desk, Renee has a catch-all bulletin board to help her keep track of phone numbers, computer passwords, project notes, and so on. She refers to it constantly and loves having so many important items easily accessible—without adding clutter to her workspace.

CHAPTER 16

SPOTLIGHT ON

Stacy Julian

SCRAPBOOKER AND
FOUNDING EDITOR OF
SIMPLE SCRAPBOOKS MAGAZINE

WHAT INSPIRES HER

"Where don't I get my inspiration? Truly, ideas come at me from all
over. I am particularly fond of housewares and product packaging,
and I certainly take inspiration from other scrapbookers—my
goodness, have you met my team?"

RELATIONSHIPS
NATURE
DAISIES
DECORATIVE NAPKINS
BRIGHT AND ENERGETIC COLORS
INSPIRATIONAL QUOTES
STRIPES
POLKA DOTS
GINGHAM

STACY JULIAN is the
founding editor of *Simple
Scrapbooks* magazine. Her
most recent book, *The
Big Picture: Scrapbook
Your Life and a Whole
Lot More,* shares her
liberating approach to
capturing and sharing
memories. Stacy's passion
for scrapbooking is matched
by her love of teaching;
she thrives on sharing her
enthusiasm and creativity
with others. She recently
launched the first website
solely dedicated to online
scrapbooking education—
bigpicturescrapbooking.com.
Stacy and her husband,
Geoff, keep busy raising
their four boys and newly
adopted daughter in Liberty
Lake, Washington.

DEDICATED TO CREATIVITY

As a professional scrapbooker, Stacy has more product
than most people would know what to do with. But she
has created a beautiful scrapbook room to house all of her
inspiring products in a way that fits her creative approach.
In the center of Stacy's space is a large island with storage
drawers and a large work surface. Throughout the rest
of her space, she stores her supplies (some visible, some
hidden) in containers that are both fun and functional.

WALL OF ALPHABETS

Stacy likes to combine different styles of
alphabets on her layouts, so she sorts them by letter
instead of by coordinated collection and stores them in
individual drawers in an apothecary-style shelf on her
wall. This organization method makes perfect sense for
Stacy's mix-and-match style. When she wants her letters
to match, she opts for stamps instead.

"My space is a reflection of me, both my personality and my creativity. As much as I admire some scrapbook spaces that I have seen and as much as I admire the scrapbookers who work in them, I know what I like and what will work for me. I think too many people see what someone else is doing and automatically assume it will work for them too."

STORING BY COLOR

Since Stacy's scrapbooking process is primarily driven by color, she organizes most of her products by color to make finding the right materials easy. She stores color-sorted cardstock, patterned paper, and sticker sheets in filing drawers within her scrapbooking island. This setup provides a one-stop shop for the fundamental supplies she needs when beginning a page.

Stacy keeps other frequently used items, like ribbon, brads, paint, and dimensional letters, in various containers within arms' reach of her scrapbooking island.

Stacy organizes her vast array of brads by color too. To keep them organized and accessible, she stores them in magnetic mini buckets that stand upright within a drawer in her work island—thanks to magnets along the bottom of the drawer.

Stacy maintains ten color drawers for embellishments and products that don't fit in her filing system. Each clear, plastic drawer contains a smaller plastic drawer filled with an assortment of little embellishments. Larger embellishments (often still in their original packaging) also fit in the bigger drawer. This system helps Stacy get a lot done because all of her supplies are organized to fit the way she works.

REFERENCE AND INSPIRATION

In one corner of Stacy's space sits a big reading chair—comfy and inviting. Nearby is a small collection of her favorite, timeless reference books and magazines. And don't forget her dish of brightly colored jelly beans—the perfect treat for cozying up with a good scrapbook magazine.

PHOTO STORAGE

Stacy maintains a unique system of chronologically and thematically organized photos—all stored in photo albums and photo boxes. Organizing and storing this way supports her process by allowing her to easily find what she needs for a given project.

MUSIC/MEMORY ROOM

Stacy loves to display the albums and projects she has created throughout her home. In fact, she has an entire room dedicated to the memories she's recorded. She stores completed albums on accessible shelves so her family can enjoy her hobby too!

SECTION

3

PROJECT BY PROJECT

Now that you've decided how to sort and store your scrapbooking stash, how about making a fun project or two to spice up your organizing efforts? We've created a variety of useful projects for our own spaces—items we hope will inspire you to create personalized projects that fit your needs and your space.

Album Labels

After spending so much time on your layouts, why would you want to store them in a plain, unadorned album? This simple approach to album labeling will help you easily tag your scrapbooks so you know what's inside before you even open them.

MATERIALS

- chipboard album
- Crop-a-Dile tool
- circle tags
- chipboard letters
- ribbon

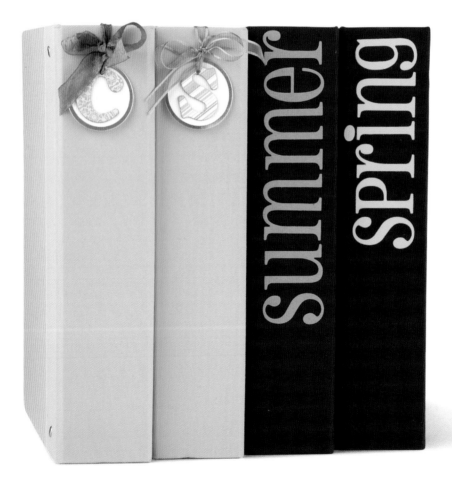

INSTRUCTIONS

① Choose a chipboard letter that corresponds with the album you're labeling and adhere it to a circle tag.

② Punch a small hole through the tag using the Crop-a-Dile tool or a handheld hole punch.

③ Using the Crop-a-Dile tool, punch a hole through your album's spine, about an inch from the top of the album.

④ Thread a piece of ribbon through the hole and tie your embellished circle tag to the album.

⑤ Display your stylishly labeled album in an accessible place so loved ones can enjoy your scrapbooking efforts.

TIP There are lots of ways to label and embellish album covers. Also try letter stickers (which may need liquid glue for extra adherence), bookplates, rub-ons, and other types of tags.

Mini Quote Book

This mini quote book will help you capture the funny and meaningful things your loved ones say. It's cute enough to be a keepsake all on its own, but it can also come in handy when it's scrapbooking time. Keep this little book on hand (maybe in your purse, maybe on the kitchen counter) so you can capture the everyday conversations you don't want to forget.

MATERIALS

- 50 3 x 5 index cards, unlined
- corner rounder (optional)
- standard hole punch
- cardstock scraps
- accents to decorate cover
- adhesive
- 1-inch jump ring
- ribbon

INSTRUCTIONS

① Use corner rounder to round the four corners of each 3 x 5 card (optional).

② Punch a hole ½-inch from the top of your first card, roughly in the center.

③ Using your first card as a guide, punch a hole in each of the remaining cards.

④ Choose cardstock for your front and back covers, and cut each to 3 x 5.

⑤ Round the cover's corners (optional) and punch a hole in each piece, using the inner pages as a guide.

⑥ Embellish the cover as desired.

⑦ Slide all cards onto the jump ring and decorate with ribbon.

⑧ Keep your quote book in an accessible location so you can use it to record journaling ideas for your scrapbooks.

 **TIP** Consider adding reinforcement labels (from your office-supply stash) to your front and back covers to protect your paper.

Photo Checklist

Thinking ahead can mean the difference between no photos of your everyday life and lots of meaningful ones. Create this photo checklist to serve as a reminder of the fun, inspiring photos you want to take each month—especially for topics that are easy to overlook (i.e., not associated with a major holiday or event).

MATERIALS

- tabbed chipboard flip album
- patterned paper
- alphabet stamp set
- journaling stamp
- white cardstock
- letter stickers
- accents to decorate cover

INSTRUCTIONS

① Cover each page with different but coordinating pieces of patterned paper.

② Stamp the name of each month on the album's label tabs.

③ Stamp journaling lines onto white cardstock and trim to size.

④ Write your photo checklist for each month along the journaling lines.

⑤ Add a letter-sticker title to each month.

⑥ Embellish the album cover with patterned paper, stickers, and stamps.

TIP If you're having trouble coming up with your photo checklists for each month, look through pictures from years past and pay attention to thoughts like, "Oh, I wish I had a picture of…"

Mini Artwork
Window Display
and Mini-album

Looking for a creative way to display your kids' artwork? Create a simple window display and mini-album to show off their artistic abilities and add a personal touch to your workspace. This simple project allows you to rotate newer artwork into your display by storing the older pictures in the associated mini-album.

WINDOW DISPLAY MATERIALS

- children's artwork
- scanner
- photo printer
- photo-quality printer paper
- laminator
- wallet-sized laminating pouches
- suction cup window display unit

MINI-ALBUM MATERIALS

- hole punch
- 1½-inch jump ring
- ribbon

INSTRUCTIONS

① Scan the selected artwork.

② Print wallet-sized scans on photo-quality printer paper.

③ Trim the scans and laminate.

④ Clip scans onto the display wire.

⑤ When you're ready to add new masterpieces into the mix, simply remove older pieces from the wire, punch a hole in each piece, and thread them onto your jump ring.

TIP If you don't have a window display unit, you can create a similar look by hanging a piece of string on a mantel or a bookcase and clipping the artwork on with clothespins.

Journal Kit

Simplify your story-writing process by storing all of your writing supplies in one place—a portable journaling basket. This easy project will make journaling more fun, more fashionable, and more faster (sorry, we couldn't help ourselves). Keeping all your journaling supplies together will help you save time searching for the supplies you need when a memorable story comes to mind.

MATERIALS

- square basket
- 2 glass jars
- your favorite journaling pens
- pencils
- pencil sharpener
- art gum eraser
- ruler
- assorted tags and pre-made journaling cards
- journaling stamps
- cardstock or patterned paper

INSTRUCTIONS

① Place both glass jars in the back of the basket.

② Put the writing tools, eraser, and ruler in one jar.

③ Fill the other jar with blank tags or cardstock pieces.

④ Create a few of your own journaling cards by stamping lines onto cardstock, patterned paper, and tags.

⑤ Place the completed journaling cards in your basket.

TIP Think about your preferred methods for gathering and saving stories (see chapter 6); then adapt this journal kit so it suits your unique process!

Inspiration Statement Board

An inspiration statement board is a visual reminder of why you scrapbook and what's most important to you. Putting your reasons for scrapbooking into words and then displaying those words in your space will offer ongoing motivation and keep your hobby centered on your highest scrapbooking priorities.

MATERIALS

- 11 x 17 chipboard
- 4 pieces of coordinating patterned paper
- assorted tags, ribbons, and cardstock scraps
- clips or other attachments
- 3 clear envelopes
- inspiring photos and magazine clippings

TIP Review chapter 2 to remind yourself of your "big-picture inspiration," or all the larger reasons you engage in this hobby.

INSTRUCTIONS

① Based on your answers to the quiz questions for Chapter 2, write a sentence that summarizes what inspires you to scrapbook.

The basic structure for your sentence should be:

"I _____ to _____."

For example, read Wendy's statement above.

Aby's statement says: "I joyfully create scrapbooks for my family to share my intense love for them and to tell the stories of our lives."

② Using the assorted materials you have gathered, add your inspiration statement to the top half of your chipboard.

③ Use clips to attach the three envelopes along the bottom of the chipboard, below your inspiration statement.

④ Write uplifting words and messages on tags and label your envelopes according to the priorities you listed in your inspiration statement.

⑤ Tuck inspiring photos and magazine clippings into the envelopes.

⑥ Display your inspiration statement in a place of prominence so you'll be continually inspired.

Magnetic Tin Labels

Keep your embellishments organized and stored together in one place with stackable magnetic tins and removable magnet labels. (That's a lot of magnets!) This labeling system is fun, simple to implement, and extremely versatile—the labels can be easily removed and reused, allowing you to change your mind about what goes in the tin.

MATERIALS

- round magnetic tins
- magnet strips, ½-inch wide
- cardstock scraps
- letter stickers

INSTRUCTIONS

① Fill tin with sorted embellishments.

② Cut magnet strips into 3–inch lengths.

③ Cut cardstock scraps to ½ x 3–inch strips.

④ Adhere cardstock strips to top of magnet strips.

⑤ Add letter stickers to create each magnet label.

⑥ Add a magnet label to each tin.

⑦ Stack 'em up and store them in your space.

TIP If you buy magnetic strips in a roll, they'll have a natural curve to them before you even add them to your tin!

Seasonal Photo Box
and Dividers

If you like to scrapbook by season, why not organize your photographs that way too? Decorate a photo box and fill it with matching dividers to spice up your photo storage and keep your pictures sorted in style all year long.

INSTRUCTIONS

① Cut cardstock to create divider cards that fit your box.

② Add seasonal titles and tab stickers to decorate the dividers.

③ Embellish photo box as desired.

④ Insert dividers into photo box.

⑤ Add seasonally sorted photos behind the appropriate dividers.

TIP This photo box idea is easy to adapt to any photo-sorting process! Just label your divider cards according to the categories you chose in chapter 4.

MATERIALS

- solid-colored photo box
- 6 sheets cardstock
- letter stickers
- tab stickers

Get-out-of-a-Rut Jar

Create this jar as a go-to solution for those days when you find yourself in a scrapbooking rut. All you have to do is pull out a piece of paper to determine the starting point for your next project or layout and—voilà!—you're on your way to a new creative creation!

MATERIALS

- glass jar
- cardstock or patterned paper
- tag punch
- ribbon

INSTRUCTIONS

① Cut 15 pieces of cardstock or paper using your selected tag punch.

② On each card, write a prompt that will require you to approach scrapbooking differently, such as:

- Start with your newest embellishment
- Design a layout with the same colors as the clothes you're wearing now
- Write a meaningful story you've been neglecting to share

③ Fold tags in half and place them in the jar.

④ Embellish the jar as desired.

⑤ Use your finished project as needed to get you out of a rut and into the creative groove.

Use your scraps to make a photo mat.

Supersize a photo / let it span the middle of two pages

Workspace Design File

A workspace design file can be a valuable tool for planning and creating your ideal scrapbooking space. It's the place to gather all of your ideas—for paint colors, furniture, canisters, and more—allowing you to carry your vision around with you as you make decisions (and purchases) for your space.

MATERIALS

- 3-ring binder
- tabs
- 3-hole punch
- plastic sheet protectors
- ideas for your space (from design books, scrapbooking magazines, home décor catalogs, paint samples, fabric swatches, etc.)

INSTRUCTIONS

① Create three tabs to organize your thoughts: "design ideas," "project ideas," and "lists/plans."

② Tear out or photocopy ideas gathered from your references.

③ Three-hole punch the ideas or slide them into sheet protectors.

④ File ideas behind the prepared tabs.

⑤ Use the binder throughout the process as you create your space, adding and adjusting as you go.

TIP Make sure you read chapter 10 to learn exactly how a design file fits into your planning process.

Resources

WELL, OUR WORK IS FINISHED HERE. WE'VE DONE EVERYTHING IN OUR POWER TO TURN YOU INTO AN ENERGIZED AND INSPIRED SCRAPBOOKING MACHINE! AND HOPEFULLY YOU'VE LEARNED A FEW NEW THINGS ABOUT YOURSELF ALONG THE WAY. IT'S GREAT TO REALIZE THAT THERE ARE COUNTLESS WAYS TO APPROACH SCRAPBOOKING—AND THAT ALL ARE PERFECTLY VALID. WOULDN'T IT BE A BORING WORLD IF WE ALL WORKED IN EXACTLY THE SAME WAY?

Each and every one of us has her own take on this fulfilling hobby—from Wendy's creative spontaneity and Aby's inspiring organization to Stacy's playful ingenuity and Beth's colorful simplicity to…however you've defined your approach. We're all unique. We each see through drastically different eyes. And isn't it fantastic?

When it comes to organizing and storing scrapbooking supplies in an inspiring and sustainable fashion, the same is absolutely true. The only "right way" is the way that motivates you to keep creating.

You are the only you there is. No one scrapbooks the way you do, which means your workspace will be (and should be!) different from everyone else's. It's up to you to determine what makes scrapbooking a fit for your life. Let your own sense of style drive you to create a space that helps you sustain this amazing hobby. Your needs, your personality, and your creative preferences are what matter, not anyone else's.

So don't be afraid to embrace what you love. Your organized and inspired workspace is just waiting to be created. Get out there and make it happen! We're behind you every step of the way.

Wendy   Aby